Justice – The Biblical Challenge

Biblical Challenges in the Contemporary World

Editor: J. W. Rogerson, University of Sheffield

Current uses of the Bible in debates about issues such as human sexuality, war and wealth and poverty often amount to either a literalist concentration on a few selected texts, or an accommodation of the Bible to secular trends. The "Biblical Challenges" series aims to acquaint readers with the biblical material pertinent to particular issues, including that which causes difficulty or embarrassment in today's world, together with suggestions about how the Bible can nonetheless present a challenge in the contemporary age. The series seeks to open up a critical dialogue between the Bible and the chosen issue, which will lead to a dialogue between the biblical text and readers, challenging them to reflection and praxis. Each volume is designed with the needs of undergraduate and college students in mind, and can serve as a course book either for a complete unit or a component.

Published:

According to the Scriptures?
The Challenge of Using the Bible in Social, Moral and Political Questions
J. W. Rogerson

The City in Biblical Perspective
J.W. Rogerson and John Vincent

The Bible and the Environment
Towards a Critical Ecological Biblical Theology
David G. Horrell

Forthcoming:

The Bible and Science: Creation
Harriet A. Harris

Science and Miracle, Faith and Doubt
A Scientific Theology of the Bible
Mark Harris

To Sara, Amy and Elisabeth

Justice – The Biblical Challenge

Walter J. Houston

Routledge
Taylor & Francis Group

LONDON AND NEW YORK

First published 2010 by Equinox, an imprint of Acumen

Published 2014 by Routledge
2 Park Square, Milton Park, Abingdon, Oxon OX14 4RN
711 Third Avenue, New York, NY 10017, USA

Routledge is an imprint of the Taylor & Francis Group, an informa business

Notices
Practitioners and researchers must always rely on their own experience
and knowledge in evaluating and using any information, methods,
compounds, or experiments described herein. In using such information
or methods they should be mindful of their own safety and the safety of
others, including parties for whom they have a professional responsibility.

To the fullest extent of the law, neither the Publisher nor the authors,
contributors, or editors, assume any liability for any injury and/or damage
to persons or property as a matter of products liability, negligence or
otherwise, or from any use or operation of any methods, products,
instructions, or ideas contained in the material herein.

British Library Cataloguing-in-Publication Data

A catalogue record for this book is available from the British Library.

ISBN   978 184553 887 3   (hardback)
          978 184553 888 0   (paperback)

Library of Congress Cataloging-in-Publication Data

Houston, Walter.
  Justice: the biblical challenge / Walter J. Houston.
    p. cm.
  Includes bibliographical references and index.
  ISBN 978-1-84553-887-3 (hb)—ISBN 978-1-84553-888-0 (pb) 1. Social justice—
Biblical teaching. 2. Bible—Criticism, interpretation, etc. 3. Social justice—Religious
aspects—Christianity. I. Title.
  BS680.J8H68 2010
  261.8—dc22
                              2010003072

Typeset by S.J.I. Services, New Delhi

Contents

PREFACE

The stimulus to write this book came from being a member of the Bible and Society Group under the leadership of John Rogerson; and the opportunity to do so resulted from our decision to take our responsibility as Christian scholars seriously by initiating a series of books reflecting on the significance of the Bible, understood critically, for Christian existence and action in modern society. This book will be the fourth to appear in this series. As far as I was concerned the group had already stimulated my many years' work on a study of social justice in the Old Testament, which appeared as *Contending for Justice* in 2006 and in a revised form in 2008. I am glad to be able to channel some of that work into a book with a broader focus and possibly a wider appeal. Naturally I have drawn pretty heavily on the insights and conclusions of my earlier book, but apart from a few short quotations which are marked as such, I have not made direct use of any material from it in this one.

I am grateful to John Rogerson for accepting the book into the series, and for what he describes as his "light touch" as an editor; "laid back" might capture his approach better. I also wish to thank Janet Joyce, our publisher, for her promptness in setting the wheels in motion, and George Moore, my copy editor, for his speedy work on the text. The greater part of the text was written in my last term of study leave from my post at Mansfield College, Oxford, and I must express my thanks once again to the Governing Body of the College for making that possible. My wife Fleur was, as ever, generous in her encouragement and eager to see the book in print. It is dedicated to our children. The challenge is to their generation, and to their own children, as much as to ours.

In writing the book I have had in mind the ordinary educated Christian, not merely the undergraduate and college student mentioned in the series preface. I have used Hebrew and Greek words as little as possible, and given them in non-technical transliterations that are intended to give some impression of the pronunciation for an English speaker rather than to correspond precisely with the original spelling.

Walter J. Houston
26 February 2010

ABBREVIATIONS

AB	Anchor Bible
BCE	before the Common Era (= bc)
CE	Common Era (= ad)
ET	English translation
JB	Jerusalem Bible
JSOTSup	Journal for the Study of the Old Testament Supplement Series
KJV	King James Version
LCL	Loeb Classical Library
LNTS	Library of New Testament Studies
NJB	New Jerusalem Bible
NRSV	New Revised Standard Version
NS	New series
ONS	Office of National Statistics
PG	*Patrologia Graeca*
REB	Revised English Bible
SOTSMS	Society for Old Testament Study Monograph Series
SWBA	Social World of Biblical Antiquity
UNU-WIDER	United Nations University World Institute for Development Economics Research
WBC	Word Biblical Commentary

Chapter 1

JUSTICE AND THE BIBLE

The Need for Justice

The subject of this book is justice, or to give it a more familiar name, fairness. Fairness is essential to all human life in society, and always has been. Is it any less so today? Suppose that we were asked what were the two greatest threats to life as we know it in the world today, many of us would name global warming and terrorism. What has fairness got to do with these? A great deal, if we want to evade the threats they pose.

To take global warming first: George Monbiot in his recent book-length analysis of possible solutions calculates that to avoid runaway global warming leading to possible ecological catastrophe we need to cut emissions of greenhouse gases worldwide by at least 60% by 2030. (This figure is probably already out of date, and calculated on the same basis it will now be even higher.) This would involve huge upheaval and pain for everyone. But different people in different parts of the world would start from very different points. Unless such cuts were *fairly* distributed, it would be impossible to reach international agreement about them. Some might suggest it would be fair for every nation to cut its emissions by 60%, thus seemingly spreading the pain evenly. But would it? Some countries have such a low standard of living already that to cut back their use of fossil fuels by 60% would impose unendurable hardships and make it impossible for their people ever to live decently. What Monbiot proposes is that the *total* emissions allowed for the world, not the cutbacks, should be divided between its countries in proportion to their population. It turns out that if that is done, the UK must reduce its emissions by 90% (way ahead of its actual plans!), while Ethiopia can increase theirs by 450%. Their peoples will then be contributing equally to the load of greenhouse gases in the atmosphere (Monbiot 2006: 16, 44). And it is precisely this kind of issue that is at the time of writing making progress so slow on the negotiations for a comprehensive carbon reduction treaty. Reaching an agreement which everyone will acknowledge as fair is pivotal to success in avoiding the breakdown of negotiations and hence the breakdown of natural world systems.

What about the threat of jihadist terrorism? The motivation of the leaders of al-Qaʻida and such groups is perhaps beyond the reach of argument. But they appeal to the generality of Muslims worldwide through the perceived unfairness of Western actions in the Middle East, particularly the support of Israel, which is seen as unbalanced and uncritical, and the unprovoked attack on Iraq. "Wars on terror" are hardly ever won by military action alone, but by ensuring that the terrorists have no support. This is only possible if the targets of terrorist attack are seen as acting fairly. Obviously the West has a very long way to go to achieve this.

These two examples are illustrations of how thoroughly the question of justice is entwined with all situations of human interaction and conflict. More specifically, they show how the injustice of the current world order, as well as being a profound problem in itself, makes it harder to solve other problems. Material resources and power are largely monopolized by a part of the world population while others have very little of either, and the inequality is increasing. Within an individual country such as the UK, there may be the same effect. The result is a divided society that is unable to perceive itself as a single community. We shall return to this in more detail in Chapter 7.

Ideas of Justice

The word "justice" is used in a variety of different ways and connections. A basic distinction that philosophers since Aristotle have made is between *distributive* and *commutative* justice (Aristotle 1939: 266–67 [*Nicomachean Ethics* V. ii. 12–13 (1130b–1131a)]). Distributive justice is concerned with the fair sharing of things, such as material resources, or work, or power or status, over society as a whole. Commutative justice is concerned with fair exchange between individuals, whether in buying and selling, or, usually under the name of *retributive* justice, in giving people what they deserve for what they have done, such as punishment for crimes or honours for benefits to society. This book will be concerned mainly with distributive justice, but we shall occasionally look at retributive justice.

Again, we can speak of justice or fairness as a personal virtue ("a beast, but a just beast" is how a nineteenth-century Rugby schoolboy described his headmaster Thomas Arnold), as a characteristic of an institution or a procedure or an outcome ("a fair trial", "fair trade", "a fair day's work for a fair day's pay"), or as a quality of a society as a whole ("we are working for a just society"). In the latter two cases the question may arise who should be held responsible for ensuring that the institution or the procedure is fair or the society is just.

People disagree, often profoundly, over what is fair in particular cases, or what may be meant by a just society. In retributive justice, some may hold that "an eye for an eye" is the definition of fairness, so that the taking of life should always be punished with death, while others would say that the death penalty can never be fair, as it ignores the possibility that a mistake has been made and eliminates any hope for repentance and reform. In the distribution of material resources, the ideal for some is equality in all things, while others hold that the only fair approach is to let the market decide how much each person's contribution is worth.

Michael Sandel gives an accessible review and assessment of many of the leading theories about justice (Sandel 2009). He shows that disagreements about justice reflect differences over the good things that we value. Deterrence, rehabilitation and appropriate punishment may all be objects of the criminal justice system, but different people give them very different weights in relation to each other. The French Revolution adopted the slogan "Liberty, equality and fraternity"; but since 1789 liberty and equality have generally been promoted by opposing political forces, while "fraternity" has perhaps been forgotten. (It may have made a recent comeback under the name of "community".) And what is meant by liberty, or freedom, may be very different in the thought of different groups. To some it means freedom from coercion and bureaucratic regulation, so that the market can operate freely. To others it means freedom from subservience. This was the understanding of freedom in the mind of R. H. Tawney when he observed many years ago, "Freedom … is not only compatible with conditions in which all men are fellow-servants, but would find in such conditions its most perfect expression. What it excludes is a society where only some are servants, while others are masters" (Tawney 1964: 166).

The same goes for equality. Aristotle gave one sense of justice as sharing equally with equals (Aristotle 1939: 268–69 [*Nicomachean Ethics* V.iii. 5–6 (1131a)]). But he needed to put it in that way because he did not believe that all people were equal. Women were inferior to men, and some men and women were "natural slaves" who should not be treated in the same way as those who were "naturally free" (Aristotle 2000: 32–34 [*Politics* I.5 (1254a–1255a)]). But people today, most of whom do believe that everyone is equal in some sense, do not necessarily agree on what this should mean. To some, people should be enabled to share the goods of this life in broadly equal measure ("equality of outcomes"). But when Americans (especially) affirm their belief that every person is equal, they mean that everyone has the same value, or is "equal in the sight of God" ("equality of status"), and that everyone has an equal chance to reach the White House or run General Electric ("equality of opportunity").

Thus although everyone believes in justice, and one can observe how the youngest child has a sense of fairness, it is nonetheless controversial. What you believe about justice, what you believe justice is, differs according to your upbringing and education, but pretty plainly also according to your economic and social position, your self-interest, and the opinions of the people you mix with. None of these things absolutely determines what you believe, but a banker in the City of London is more likely to believe that market outcomes are fair than a car worker who has lost his job, and a successful businessman is less likely to believe in equality of outcomes than a trade unionist. People may have a set of beliefs, perhaps supported by little stories (like the "log cabin to White House" story in America), which serves to justify their understanding of justice, sometimes in the face of the facts (cf. Newsom 2003: 122–23). When this understanding also supports their own social position or aspirations, I shall call their ideas an *ideology*. Some ideologies, arising from a particular group, succeed in dominating whole societies, as Marxist ideology dominated Eastern Europe before 1989, and as the ideology of the market and equality of opportunity dominates the USA today.

Justice and the Bible

The Bible, as we shall see, has a good deal to say about justice. But does it have anything useful to contribute to our present-day discussions about justice? And, if we believe it does, what degree of authority should it have? The important recent examination of the idea of justice by Amartya Sen (Sen 2009, reflecting a large body of earlier work by himself and others), may suggest that relying on the authority of an ancient religious text is ill-advised. His initial point is that we arrive at the best idea of what is just through reasoning and discussion, in as open a circle as possible (Sen 2009: 31–52, 124–52). Appealing to authority is the antithesis of open discussion. Sen himself refers to an ancient religious text, the *Bhagavadgita* (Sen 2009: 208–17), and more than once to the practice of Indian rulers of former times. But he does not use these as authorities to which he defers, more as contributors to the discussion. It is rather in this way that I wish to use the Bible in this book, as I will explain.

There are two extreme positions which some, perhaps many, people reading this book may hold, but which I would want to distance myself from. One view is that documents written 2000 years ago or more cannot have anything useful to say to us today, since they were written in societies very different from those of today, which faced none of our problems, and are governed by an outdated and incredible world view. The other is that because the Bible is the Word of God, anything it says about any subject is of absolute authority and anyone who claims to be a Christian must obey it implicitly.

To take the latter of these two views first, the plain fact is that neither on this subject nor on most others is there one unanimous view in the Bible. This is shown very clearly by John Rogerson in his contribution to this series (Rogerson 2007: 1–7). To take an example not dealt with by Rogerson, there are two very different attitudes to kingship in the Bible. While some of the Psalms give a very high status to the king as the "son" of God (Ps. 2:7; 89:26) and his personal agent on earth (the same psalms, with 110 and others), Deuteronomy (17:14–20) seeks to limit his power and makes it clear that he is only one among many "brothers", is not to exalt himself above them (v. 20), and is to have the words of the Law set above *him* (v. 19). That is not to say that these views cannot be reconciled, but interpreters who wish to do that must decide which are the key texts and implicitly relativize others, or interpret them in a different way (for example, by applying the Psalms to the Messiah). Then, further, they have the problem of deciding how they are to be applied in the completely different social and political context of today. This leaves someone holding this view in a position not very different from that of a believer who values the Bible without attributing such absolute authority to it.

There may be even greater difficulty with things on which the whole Bible is agreed. There is no part of the Bible which does not accept slavery as a fact of life, or which in any way criticizes people for holding slaves. Certainly you can derive an argument against slavery from things that the Bible does say; but you cannot then consistently attribute authority to the texts which imply slavery is permissible. You might perhaps argue that they were authoritative to those who first heard them, and that God always has "more truth and light yet to break forth out of his holy Word", in the words which John Robinson is supposed to have used to the departing "pilgrims" on the Mayflower in 1620. The latter point is profoundly true: it is indeed true that those who fought against slavery in the British Empire and in the United States in the eighteenth and nineteenth centuries were inspired by the Bible though not by anything the Bible specifically says about slavery. But the texts which permit slavery are so thoroughly accepting of the current social conditions and the self-interest of slave-owners that it is almost blasphemous, in my view, to say that they must be the word of God.

In other words, we cannot simply accept everything the Bible says on this (or any other) subject. The words of the Bible are always the words of human beings, and I would argue that the points I have just made show that they are not always inspired by God. If we are to determine how God nevertheless speaks to us in it, we have to approach it with discernment and critical reflection. We must decide what we take to be the broad underlying thrust of biblical teaching. This is inevitably a subjective decision: any two readers may answer the question in different ways. Then the question arises: is the text I am reading in accord with that broad thrust, and if not, how am I to understand it? As we shall see later, we may often have to allow for the self-interest of the writers or their class creeping into the text. And how am I to bring together what I find in the Bible with what I know of society today and other influences on my ethical stance? – influences which we all have, whether we realize it or not. For example, how am I to reconcile my cheerful acceptance of interest payments on my savings, and my knowledge that credit, with the associated interest charges, enables a modern economy to work, with the Bible's unanimous condemnation of the charging of interest? Muslims, after all, refuse to make such a reconciliation, but there is little sign that many Christians want to go down that route. For a useful discussion, see Rogerson 2007: 95–98.

That brings us to the argument that the Bible's remoteness in time and cultural context must make it irrelevant to us today. Cyril Rodd (2001), for example, entitles his book on Old Testament ethics *Glimpses of a Strange Land*, and compares the experience of studying the ethics of the Old Testament to that of ascending an old tower with a spiral staircase and narrow slit windows in a strange country. The landscape is strange, and we only get glimpses of it now and again in the limited material the text offers us.

The weight of this argument should not be underestimated. It is not only the social background of the Bible that appears to make it irrelevant to our situation, but technology and politics as well. Isaiah had never seen a factory or driven a car; Nehemiah knew nothing of parliamentary democracy. But it is the fundamental difference in the economy, social structure and culture which really appears to put the Bible out of court for our modern Western situation. It was written in a community where the great majority of the population lived in small towns or villages and engaged in agriculture, where for most people the work unit was the family, where professions were inherited, where marriage was a contract between families in which the bride and groom had little say, where slavery and concubinage were accepted practices, where women took no part in public life and old men exercised authority over everyone descended from them.

This, or something like it, is true not only of the Bible but of all old texts; yet people go on reading them, and not simply for pleasure or curiosity. Philosophers still read Plato and Aristotle; Sandel is indebted to Aristotle (384–322 BCE) for much of his argument (Sandel 2009: 184–207), just as Sen uses the *Bhagavadgita*. Communication between the past and the present (though not the other way round!) is a reality. Can we actually learn something from the past? There has been a good deal of thinking about this. The image that Hans-Georg Gadamer offers is that of "the merging of horizons" (Gadamer 1989: 302–05). We call the limit of everything that we can see on the ground the horizon. But everyone's horizon is different, because everyone stands in a different place. Gadamer uses this idea as a metaphor in talking about the "standpoints" of written texts and their readers. Everything that you know and every activity you take part in is your "world", and its limit is your "horizon", which depends on your "standpoint". If you read a text, it has a horizon too, different from yours, because the writer's standpoint and the writer's "world" are different; but, because the writer is a human being, and especially if you stand in the same philosophical or religious tradition as the writer, not so completely different that you cannot understand what it is talking about. Gadamer argues that in the effort to understand a text properly, we first of all transpose ourselves into its horizon, and then we find that our own horizon and the horizon of the text "merge" so that we find ourselves with a new and broader horizon within which to understand our own world.

This is a process that we are familiar with in everyday life. Take the case of a young person brought up in an affluent British middle-class home who goes to India in her "gap year", and is stunned by the presence everywhere of grinding poverty side by side with ostentatious affluence. This awakens her to the fact that stark inequality also exists in Britain, though it tends to be invisible unless you are looking for it, because the poor are hidden away on council estates (public housing projects). She might have been aware of that already, of course. But she still will have something to learn from the ingenuity of the Indian poor in making the best of what they have, wringing livelihood out of the tiniest scraps of stuff that in this country go from the house to the bin (trashcan) to landfill. She might learn that the poor do not need to be victims, or simply the object of charity or welfare payments; that they can take charge of their own destiny.

There is no guarantee that the new horizon will always contribute much of significance to understanding our own world. Nor is the merging of horizons something we can expect to happen automatically: it is the result of hard study and reflection. Can we approach that task in a way that makes it more likely that the merging of horizons will be fruitful for our understanding of our "world" and our own action within it?

First of all, we need to realize that in reading the Bible we are not like archaeologists who have dug up some texts, thousands of years old, and have just learnt to decipher and read them. We are not looking back from the twenty-first century to the time of the Bible over an empty abyss. On the contrary, we are heirs to a rich tradition of interpretation which has gone on over 2000 years and more. This is in large measure the message of Rogerson (2007). We belong to communities of Jews and Christians who have constantly been reading the Scriptures and making interpretations of them, and theological libraries are full of their commentaries. We find it much easier to "transpose" ourselves into the "horizon" of the biblical writings because the tradition in which we stand forms as it were a continuous chain of horizons, "merging" gradually into each other.

The only problem arises when we mistake this tradition of interpretation for the original horizon of the biblical writers. People tend to think that they are reading a passage in its plain obvious sense when in fact they are following the interpretation of long-dead theologians. A good example is when people call the story in Genesis 3 "the Fall of man" (I purposely use their language!). Would anyone who knew nothing of Christianity and was handed the chapter to read come up with those words as a description of the event? I doubt it. But there is nothing wrong in following an old interpretation, provided we realize that that is what we are doing; on the contrary, our reading is deepened and enriched by all the work that has been done before.

One popular way of proceeding is to deduce from particular prescriptions and assertions of the Bible, which can only apply as such to the ancient society in which they were written, general principles which can be applied to our own society by way of "middle axioms" (Temple 1941: 10; Preston 1976: 7–8). This is a lot harder than it looks. The central problem is that in the abstract one cannot tell which of many possible general principles are the ones which ought to be derived, or how we ought to determine this (Schluter and Clements 1986: 48–49). The selection of principles, and their interpretation, are at the mercy of the moral and political prejudices of the interpreter. This is especially so if they are too general – for example, "Justice ought to be pursued in all social relationships". We have already seen that justice may mean any number of different things, and that how it is understood often depends on a person's social position and political beliefs. If all that the Bible is able to offer us is such broad principles, there is a risk that readers might find nothing in it that they did not already believe. There would be no genuine "merging of horizons" if the modern horizon simply overwhelmed the biblical one.

On the other hand, if we wish to be more precise, then we may find ourselves landed with a principle that is indeed much closer to the distinctive view of some biblical passage, but cannot obviously be applied in our very different world. For example, we might conclude that the key principle to be taken from Leviticus 25 is that all economic assets should be periodically redistributed among the population. Would that be any help in the world we live in, with its existing economic systems and property laws? It would require a revolution to institute, and one cannot even begin to talk about revolution without some idea of how it would happen, who would carry it out – and how the mess would be cleared up.

Rather than this derivation of abstract principles in isolation, Christopher J. H. Wright, who is concerned with the Old Testament in particular, prefers to think of ancient Israel as a "paradigm" for the social life of humanity in general under God (Wright 2004: 63–73). By this he means that the whole life of Israel (as presented in the OT) in its concrete particularity is a pattern that suggests the principles which may apply to the life of other societies, provided that they are seen as a total package in their particular setting.

> To regard Israel and the Old Testament as an ethical paradigm forces us constantly to go back to the hard given reality of the text of the Bible itself and imaginatively to live with Israel in their world, before returning to the equally hard given reality of our own world, to discover imaginatively how that paradigm challenges our ethical response there. (Wright 2004: 71)

This approach embodies two very important points. One is that ethical rules and systems and habits never exist in a vacuum, but have to be seen in relation to the real life of the society in which they arose. This is fundamental to the way I shall be looking at biblical texts in this book, and in the next chapter I shall try to sketch out how I understand the social history of the societies in which the biblical documents were written and to which their writers addressed themselves. However, there is an important difference between the way Wright does this and the way I shall do it. Wright uses the laws and early narratives of the Bible as a whole to create his picture of the social reality of Israel, which then becomes the pattern which challenges our world. Along with most critical scholars, I believe it is misleading to combine all the laws into a single picture which is then presented as the historical reality, because they come from different periods and were never all applied at the same time – if they were applied at all. The social reality of "Israel" is difficult to reconstruct at any historical period (see Grabbe 2007). Even the archaeological evidence is ambiguous, while the texts, rather than defining the historical reality, suggest a picture of a social "world" which is often idealized, or even fantasized (as in the story of Job), while the prophets often go to the opposite extreme and exaggerate the corruption of their society (e.g. Jer. 5:1–5). But although the biblical texts do not present a reliable picture of their world, they do arise out of the real world, and often challenge it, and it is these words that challenge our world, just as they challenged the world of ancient Israel.

Wright's other sound point is that all attempts to apply ancient texts to modern society, or to set up a dialogue between them, require the use of our imagination. There is no rule for doing it that can be worked out rationally and applied logically. The Bible's challenge is at least as much through its images and metaphors as through its laws and rules. This is a point I shall return to.

The liberation theologians of Latin America (and elsewhere) take a rather different line. They are convinced that the Bible makes it very clear what justice is, and challenges us today to do justice. Their characteristic standpoint is that the Gospel, the story of the Exodus, the story of Jesus, the story of God's liberation, is heard by the poor, and by those who stand with them, as the story of the poor. If we cannot hear what the Bible has to say to us, according to them, it is not because we live in a different *cultural* world, but because we do not stand where the Bible stands *morally*, on the side of the oppressed poor. Such oppression is still going on today. The fact that it takes different forms today does not matter from a moral point of view. "The capitalism criticized by Marx is only the last link (we hope) in a long chain of oppression", says José Miranda (1977: xviii). So generally this school of writers displays little interest in the precise social backgrounds of biblical texts. As long as it is clear that the Bible is attacking oppression which extracts profit from the poor, it is no different from oppression today. We evade this point because we are ourselves implicated in exploiting the poor, even if only indirectly, and do not want to hear that justice means nothing other than stopping what we are doing to them. In the UK Tim Gorringe (1994) takes up a very similar position. If we follow this line, the antiquity and strangeness of the Bible do not matter so much. We treat it not as an impersonal textbook from which principles may be derived by an intellectual process, but personally and practically, as the word of the living God which calls us to practise justice.

As we shall see, there are other aspects to justice in the Bible besides this vitally important one. But in any case there may be a problem with the way writers such as Miranda have formulated it. Is it actually true that the Bible is always against oppression and for the poor? Some writers who are close to the liberation theologians in moral, political and theological terms take a much more suspicious view of the text. They insist that one has to take into account that almost all, if not all, the writers of the Bible would have come from the upper classes. Working people would not have had the leisure or the necessary education to be able to compose the kind of books which make up our Bible. Itumeleng Mosala, a black South African scholar, maintains that the Bible is largely the work of dominant groups in society, and represents their ideology. As a Marxist, he believes that class conflict is basic to all civilized societies, and anything produced in such a situation will reflect it. Since written works coming out of ancient Israel and the Roman world will have been written by members of the classes who were able to write, that is the upper classes, they will generally represent their view of the conflict.

Of course, Mosala does not stop at such a priori considerations. For him, the proof that, in general, this is true of biblical texts lies in the fact that the apartheid regime in South Africa was able to use texts from the Bible to support their domination and oppression of black South Africans. "My contention", says Mosala, "is that the only adequate and honest explanation is that not all of the Bible is on the side of human rights or of oppressed and exploited people" (Mosala 1989: 30). There are some texts in the Bible that support the oppressed (Mosala does not clearly explain why they are there), but many that do not, such as the story of the dispossession of the native population of Canaan by the Israelites, or the many texts in the prophets which look forward to the restoration of the fortress of Zion, the seat of the rulers and officials of Judah in Jerusalem.

Mosala's work is too heavily under the influence of a dogmatic Marxism, which leads him to assert what *must* be true, for example that the texts of the Bible reflect class conflict, rather than first looking at the evidence. We shall be looking at some of the evidence later on. All the same, he makes some points that are undeniable, and others that are worth exploring. It is undeniable that educated people with enough resources to have leisure to write must have written the texts of the Old and New Testaments. It is undeniable that when they wrote about justice they were writing in real social situations, and were trying to influence and persuade other people, who may have disagreed: that is certainly obvious in the prophets. It is worth exploring to what extent our texts represent the viewpoint and interests of the upper classes. This is what I have done at some length for the Old Testament in my book *Contending for Justice* (Houston 2008), and I shall be using some of the results later on in this book.

It is obviously important to make out whether the Bible taken as a whole witnesses to the God who delivers the oppressed, as the liberation theologians assert, or expresses the attitudes and interests of their oppressors. What Mosala does not allow for is that not all the attitudes of upper class people, especially those who put pen to paper, support oppression. They may sympathize with the poor. They may wish to protect them. A sense of *noblesse oblige* is widespread, though certainly not universal, among aristocrats in traditional societies: that is, the belief that being privileged means that you owe something to the people who depend on you. For the Bible we have to take religious motivation into account. The God of Israel is consistently seen as a god of justice, though we must realize that even in the Bible that word has many different connotations (Knierim 1995: 89–114; Houston 2008; for God's justice ib. 204–19). As I have shown in my earlier book (Houston 2008: 13–15), even a ruling group's desire to protect and justify its position by ideological writing may involve it in accepting the rightful claims of subordinate groups and individuals for a fair share of society's resources. For ideologies make claims to be universally and unquestionably true, and they can only be seen in this way if they embody the social, moral and religious ideas which people in general in a particular society accept as true. This opens up the interesting possibility that a text may take for granted the dominant position of certain people while at the same time the moral ideas which it works with bring domination and inequality radically into question. In *Contending for Justice* I showed this in respect of, at least, Deut. 15:1–18 and some wisdom texts (Houston 2008: 180–90 (cf. Houston 1999); 118–31). If we want to say that God speaks to us in these words, it is not because they come from a divine standpoint over against all human affairs, but rather that we discern what God says in and through the words and struggles of people who have their own sometimes self-regarding agendas and motivations, but witness to the justice of God willy-nilly.

Let me draw out a couple of the practical ways in which the Bible assists us in thinking about the theme of justice, in its broadest range of senses, setting aside all talk of principles and paradigms, and at the same time taking seriously the difference of horizons between the worlds of the Bible and our own worlds today (both of them plural!)

First, most of the texts of the Bible are imaginative literature, not systematic reflection: poetry, narrative, vision, parable. Thought about how readers relate to such literature can be useful. David Clines argues that: "A literary text creates an alternative 'world', another set of principles, values, relationships, and perceptions, which then confronts the reader … The world thus created invites the reader to enter it" (Clines 1976: 54). The newness, the challenging character, of such a world will strike even the contemporary reader, not only one of a later time. Clines is here speaking of such works as poems and novels. But the same may be true of a wide range of works marked by the use of the imagination. A text such as Leviticus 25, on the jubilee, or Isa. 5:1–7, the song of the vineyard, or Revelation 21, the new Jerusalem, is a work of the imagination, a literary work in Clines's sense, which creates a world of its own. I do not mean by this that what it conveys is imaginary in the sense of unreal or fantastic. Rather, it grasps the solid reality of God's justice and expresses it imaginatively, in a form which can be grasped in its turn through the imagination of the reader who enters its world. Not necessarily through imagery, though images are significant – the ram's horn which is sent round to proclaim liberty, the vineyard bringing forth wild grapes, the leaves of the tree for the healing of the nations … But a detailed programme of laws worked out as we have it in Leviticus 25 is equally a work of the imagination, taking a single decisive idea and working out what it would mean in legal and moral terms. Such an imaginative world may call into question the cruelty, injustice or failure of the existing social world. The song of the vineyard in Isaiah 5 does this explicitly, but it may equally well be implicit. The practical significance of a "utopian" text such as Leviticus 25, or an "eschatological" one such as Revelation 21 is that it embodies a deliberate alternative to current social practice, challenging its cruelty and injustice with the mercy and justice of God, in a specific rather than a general form, a form which can be understood, remembered and looked to for inspiration regardless of whether it seems realistic in the world we know, the unreformed and unconverted world.

To read such a text and seek seriously to understand it, regardless of whether the reader is a contemporary of the writing or lives in a later age, is to experience the tension between the ideal and the "reality", the world as it is and the world as it ought to be. The horizon of the text, which is defined by this tension, merges with the horizon of any readers who are aware of the same tension in their own world, and so they find that the text illuminates and judges their world. This does not depend ultimately on the perception of parallels and paradigms or on the analysis of moral principles, though serious intellectual work is needed to understand all such aspects of the text. It depends rather on the response of the imagination to the moral feeling evoked by the text, which is called forth in the same way by our own context.

As one might expect, the ideas we have to work with in reading the Bible for inspiration are not just moral but also theological. Biblical texts on justice regularly call on God as the protector of the oppressed and the guarantor of justice in the human world: the redeemer of Israel and the one who comes to judge the earth with righteousness (Ps. 96:13; 98:9). As I have already noted, there is not just one idea of God's justice in the Bible: the two ideas I have just mentioned, of the redeemer of *Israel* and the judge of the *world*, do not always fit together smoothly, but can clash quite sharply, as when for Israel's sake the former inhabitants of the holy land are violently deprived of it (Knierim 1995: 96–100; Houston 2008: 208–11). Moreover, any idea of God as just is challenged in the Bible itself, as the books of Job and Ecclesiastes reflect on the counter-evidence. However, despite these problems, the theology of justice in the texts we shall study must affect the way in which we ourselves understand them theologically. I suggest that we need to understand them as speaking about a reality which we can define in both human and theological terms. Humanly speaking, it is the effort of human beings in all ages to establish justice. In theological terms, I have defined it as "the action of God to create a just, peaceful and blessed human community" (Houston 2008: 15). This community goes under various names: in the Gospels it is the kingdom of God, in the book of Isaiah it is Zion, in the book of Revelation it is the new Jerusalem. The texts are a response to this action of God, and an expression of the human work for justice that God's action incites. And it is essential to our interpretation that this action can be traced and this work goes on *today*, wherever the good news of God's righteousness is preached. Interpreting a biblical text on justice means identifying the part that the text plays in the work for justice in the ancient context, and then using our imagination to open up its critical and constructive potential for today.

The other way in which readers may be related to the Bible text is complementary to this. We have been speaking of the text as a work of the imagination which hits its readers as something new. But of course in reality that is the exception rather than the rule, though ideally one could hope that whenever anyone reads or hears a passage they find something new in it. Most Bible readers have known it for a long time; they may read it regularly; they hear it read in the gathering of the Jewish or Christian community; and they have become very familiar with many passages. This familiarity need not breed contempt, but should rather enable the community and its members to become soaked in the text and its themes, its images and its morality. People are shaped to an extent by the stories they hear and the instruction that they receive. This is true in particular of what they hear in community, which defines what it means to belong to that community (Hauerwas 1981). Over time, regular and faithful reading (or hearing – for what we are talking about is not tied to literacy or education) in the community of the faithful forms character. Character may be defined as the tendency in a person towards particular kinds of conduct which is developed and strengthened by habit, good or bad. This is not the place to enter into the nature-nurture argument about whether character is formed more by people's genetic inheritance or by their upbringing, but simply to suggest that, among the manifold influences in which an upbringing consists, not the least important, in a religious community, is the community's scriptures.

Stanley Hauerwas speaks of communities, and the character of their members, being formed by stories (Hauerwas 1981). "Character is formed in response to stories told in community" (Bondi 1984: 201). Hauerwas argues that the story of Jesus, understood as the coming of the kingdom of God, *is* the essential Christian social ethic (Hauerwas 1981: 36–52). And the first responsibility of the church in the field of social ethics is to ensure that the church itself is formed in accordance with this story, or, as he puts it, "to be herself" (Hauerwas 1981: 84). Bruce Birch applies this insight to the Old Testament by arguing that the Exodus is the community-forming story of Israel (Birch 1995). This makes the Old Testament centre on the story of the exodus in the same way as the New Testament centres on the story of Jesus. I am doubtful whether this is a proper parallel. What we can say more safely is that the Jewish community is shaped by the Torah *as a whole* – the instruction as well as the story – in the same way as the Christian community is shaped by the Gospels, which also include instruction, though their primary purpose is to present the story (see van Wijk-Bos 2005).

For our purpose, the question needs to be asked whether, in what sense and to what extent these shaping scriptures propound justice. Are they fitted to create just communities? Sen (2009: 5–27) distinguishes between theories that set out what an ideally just society would look like or how it might be achieved in the abstract, which do not agree with each other, and ones, which he prefers, that aim to see how society as it exists might be more just, or less unjust. There is little or nothing of the former in the Bible, even though some texts may be called "utopian"; but stories which create character may help to promote justice in the world as we know it. The touchstone of justice in the Bible is relationship. It is good relationships, fair, honest and faithful, which constitute justice. But different relationships may carry different, or even clashing, responsibilities.

We have already noted the prominence of the exodus in liberation theology. For this strand of theology the deliverance of Israel from Egypt is the paradigm of God's response to the cry of the oppressed, therefore the story of justice *par excellence.* More specifically, for Jewish hearers, it is the paradigm of God's faithfulness to Israel, and this also is a form of justice: it is fulfilling one's obligations to those to whom one is committed (cf. Sen 2009: 160), a commitment expressed formally by covenant (Houston 2008: 210–14; see also Levenson 1993). Moreover, the fact that the Israelites were slaves and aliens in Egypt and were delivered from there by God is appealed to again and again in the instructional material in the Torah as a motive for Israelites to do justice to aliens, their slaves and the poor in general who depend upon them. This happens in the version of the Sabbath commandment in Deut. 5:15: "… that your slaves, male and female, may rest like you. You shall remember that you were a slave in Egypt, and YHWH your God rescued you from there with a strong hand and an outstretched arm; therefore YHWH your God commands you to keep the Sabbath day."[1] In this use of the exodus theme "Israel", that is, those intended to hear the words of the Torah, are seen to be in Hauerwas's sense a community shaped by story. Their narrated experience, the story repeated at every Passover, defines the way in which they are to behave towards those in their power. The prophetic reproaches in Jer. 2:4–13, Amos 2:9–10 and Mic. 6:1–5 take up the theme and accuse their hearers of failure to remember this experience or to apply it rightly to their own conduct. And large parts at least of the Torah, regardless of whether the exodus is mentioned, can be seen as instruction in justice, for example Exodus 21–23.

However, the idea of the justice of God in the story of the exodus is not without its problems. As I have noted in *Contending for Justice*, what is

1. "YHWH" is how I shall consistently render the personal name of the God of Israel, which was eventually regarded as too holy to be pronounced aloud. The spelling represents the four consonants of the Hebrew text. The supposed ancient pronunciation was "Yahweh", which is found in the JB and NJB, and in many scholarly works. Most English Bible versions render the name as "the LORD" in small capitals.

justice for the Israelites turns out to be injustice for the Canaanites, and before that for many Egyptians (Houston 2008: 207–11). This is the classic example of a clash of two concepts of divine justice: the universal kingly justice that brings order and peace to the world as a whole, and the particular patronal justice that responds to the needs of those to whom God (YHWH) is personally bound as redeemer (Houston 2008: 205–22). The deliverance of Israel is justice in terms of the particular, that is, in the terms within which the story is told: Egypt is the enemy, therefore all Egyptians are fair game; Canaanites occupy the land designated for Israel (Exod. 3:8), and would be a spiritual danger to Israel if permitted to survive there (Deut. 7:4, 16, 25–26). But it ceases to be just if measured by the yardstick of universal justice, which aims to moderate the claims of all without favouritism. But this is a yardstick which is foreign to the story, though it is well established elsewhere in the Torah (e.g. Deut. 10:17–18). To denounce God's conduct in this story as unjust is an oversimplified response which does not take account of what ancient readers, as well as many modern ones, would understand as justice. We shall return to this in Chapter 4.

The question is still more complex when asked of the story of Jesus, as the shaping narrative of the Christian community, or, better, Christian communities. It depends on what you mean by the story of Jesus, and how it is interpreted. Here I shall just point to two interpretive moves which can be found in the New Testament itself. One is the way in which Luke sets out the programme of Jesus' ministry as the fulfilment of Isa. 61:1–2 (plus part of Isa. 58:6: Lk 4:18–21). This makes Jesus the bearer of "good news for the poor", and proclaiming a message of liberation for prisoners of war and the oppressed, and of the "acceptable year of the Lord", which is probably a reference to the jubilee of Leviticus 25. In other words, the ministry of Jesus will set on foot the prophesied deliverance of Israel from all forms of captivity and oppression and their return to their homes. This understanding of Jesus' ministry requires working out in detail.

The other move is made by the one New Testament writing that uses the vocabulary of "justice" and related words to define what God has accomplished in Jesus: the Epistle to the Romans. "The justice of God has been revealed … through faith in Jesus Christ … to display his justice at the present time, in his being himself just and making just everyone who believes in Jesus" (Rom. 3:21–22, 26, my translation). What is the underlying concept of justice relied on by Paul here? How is it related to Old Testament concepts of justice? In what way does it encourage the community that is shaped by the story of Jesus to be just, in itself and in its members? These questions will occupy us at a later stage.

Naturally, these leading or shaping stories are not the only biblical texts that could be of significance in forming a just community and just people. We might refer to Nathan's parable in 2 Samuel 12 (and David's response), the exhortation in Amos 5:21–24, the theme of God's justice in such Psalms as 82 or 96, the exhortations to care for the poor in Proverbs, the picture of the last judgement in Matthew 25, the parable of the good Samaritan, Paul's insistence that concern for the "weaker brother" should limit a Christian's use of his or her privileges in Romans 15 or 1 Corinthians 8–10, or the vision of the new Jerusalem in Revelation 21–22. Though these passages do not all present the same ideas of justice, they can combine in the mind and memory of the faithful to form an atmosphere of fairness and justice, urging them towards right and fair conduct in their daily lives, in the way their community is structured and run, and in their ventures into the political life of the wider society.

This has been a long discussion, and it is time I wound it up and summarized the results. We cannot look to the Bible's text, taken literally, for precise guidance on what justice is or how to implement it. It is rather the formation of character and relationships, community building, challenge and inspiration that we may expect to draw from it. But that does not mean that the details of the biblical text are unimportant. On the contrary, it is precisely the details that are valuable. First, they bring to life the social context from which the text emerged. We need other evidence as well, which I will try to provide in the next chapter. This is essential in order to understand the text realistically as the work of real people addressed to an audience in a real situation; to understand the motivation of the writers as social actors with social as well as individual motives.

Second, the details may embody ideas of justice in different ways, whether through narrative, image or instruction. The exegetical task is to analyse how justice is conceived in each individual text and how this is related to the social world presupposed by the text. We need in doing that to be aware of the possible influence of the self-interest or class interest of the writers, but only so that we can distinguish those ideas that transcend those interests, that represent a tradition with deeper roots. The theological challenge is to respond to those aspects of the text that express that deeper tradition and that have shaped Jewish and Christian communities, creatively exploring how at this point in history they may shape the lives of the faithful and their religious communities, or offer a challenge to the institutions, structures and policies of the societies in which the faithful find themselves set. This is the programme that I shall try to carry out in this book.

The second chapter will attempt to give a sketch of typical relations of honour, power and wealth in four communities of the world of the Bible: the village, the state, the city and the religious community. We must conceive of our texts as speaking to situations like these, and presenting their ideals or denunciations against their background.

I shall then group the studies of texts under headings according to the overarching narrative which seems to govern them, and not according to any external categories that might be imposed upon them, nor to the issues to which they might be applied. However, in passing I shall suggest ways in which the biblical narratives, images and instruction might stimulate our imaginations in relation to the questions of justice and injustice, fairness and unfairness, of our present world. The last two chapters will be entirely devoted to application. Chapter 7 will undertake what I have called a "justice audit" of the twenty-first-century world, evaluating the world as a whole and also the society of my own nation, the United Kingdom, in the light of the different concepts of justice which emerge from our study of the texts; and the final chapter will offer suggestions for practical action.

Chapter 2

THE ANCIENT SOCIAL CONTEXTS

As I have emphasized, it is only possible to understand ideas of justice if one understands the society in which the ideas arose, the context in which the ideas made sense. This also enables one to understand the interest writers may have had in using such ideas in an ideological way, protecting the interests of their class while satisfying – at least verbally – popular demand for justice. This chapter is not concerned with the entire reality of the societies out of which the biblical books came, but with the sources of wealth, the social structure, the bonds of kinship, the concerns of honour, and the distribution of power and privilege, wealth and poverty. The equally important network of moral and religious customs, practices and ideas which form the basis of justice or the justification for injustice are in a sense the subject of the following three chapters. (For a useful and readable overview of all this, see McNutt 1999.)

Society of course changed through the centuries, but in its basic realities it changed surprisingly little. Throughout the biblical period the ultimate source of the great majority of wealth for everyone, whether they lived on the land or in the city, was agriculture and the raising of animals. Trade and industry accounted for little, even as late as New Testament times. And those who were directly concerned with winning life from the earth lived in much the same way throughout: mostly in small villages, often close to subsistence levels, generally in close-knit family groups larger than the nuclear family, and working in ways guided mainly by tradition rather than efficiency or the market. It was the institutions of the state and the city – the city which is almost always a creation of the state – laid over this essential foundation which changed more, and the impact they had on the lives of the agrarian population also varied, in ways which at times raised significant questions of justice.

I shall organize this chapter, therefore, by looking at four of the main kinds of community which existed during the time over which the biblical writings emerged, roughly speaking the middle of the eighth century BCE to the end of the first century CE: the village, the state, the city, and the religious community or sect represented by the churches to whom Paul wrote. The family is the most basic social unit, but I shall deal with that in the context of the village, because the two are closely bound up together (see also Perdue *et al.* 1997). I shall then ask what challenges to justice existed in these communities. This will form the bridge to the next chapter.

The Village

The writings of the Bible were probably all written in the cities, where the very few educated people would have lived. Some of them may reflect an oral tradition cultivated in rural society (e.g. possibly parts of the Synoptic Gospels) or its social situation (e.g. perhaps parts of Deuteronomy), but the impressions they give of rural life need to be treated with care. Recent archaeological research in Israel, partly driven by the need to salvage remains ahead of development, has begun to broaden its scope, and to look not only at the big mounds and the wealthy cities, but at the humble villages. We have thus gained significant insight into the lives of the majority, but mostly only for the early part of this period, the time of the monarchies of Israel and Judah.

For the most part, rural people did not live on their farms, but in villages of a few dozen houses and a few hundred inhabitants, going out to their work each day; rural society in the Mediterranean area has always been like this. Village houses in the monarchic period were built on a generous scale, large enough to accommodate an extended family with their animals (Faust 1999a: 243–47). The extended family (*bet ab* in Hebrew) is likely to have been the basic working unit. It would have consisted of a patriarchal head and his wife and his sons, or some of them, with their wives and children, together with servants: just such a family as in the story of the Flood goes into the ark with Noah (Gen. 7:1) (Bendor 1996; see McNutt 1999: 75–98, 164–70). The size of the houses suggests that this is also the living unit (cf. Deut. 25:5); but this must have depended on the size of the family. In the monarchic period, the people of the village as a whole regarded themselves as related, descended in the male line from a common ancestor. One or more villages made up a recognized lineage (*mishpaha* in Hebrew, sometimes called a clan). The village land would have been divided among the families of the village, probably in a number of parcels to each family in order to equalize the chances of getting good land and bad. Some have held that the land was redivided periodically (see Bendor 1996: 141–60), but there is more evidence for the continuous inheritance of land within the family. Each family would have been responsible for the cultivation of its own parcels, but the village or *mishpaha* must have worked co-operatively on installations such as silos and olive oil presses and boundary walls, which we find serving the village as a whole (Faust 2000 or Faust forthcoming for all these details).

Consistent with the villages' co-operative working is their ethos of equality and simplicity, suggested by Avraham Faust from such clues as the relatively equal size of the houses – Israelite villages contain no mansions or manor houses, nor any cottages or hovels – the undecorated pottery, and the absence of elaborate burial practices – the dead were simply laid in the earth without grave goods. An ethos of equality does not necessarily imply actual material equality, but if any families prospered especially well, it was not done to flaunt their wealth (Faust 2000: 28; 2004). Deuteronomy appeals to this rooted egalitarian feeling and kin-based solidarity when it calls fellow-Israelites "brothers" (Deut. 15:7, etc.). Rogerson argues that an egalitarian society "never existed" in ancient Israel (Rogerson 2009: 108). It is not clear that this view has been tested against the archaeological record.

It seems probable that this social structure did not, at least in its integrity, survive the fearful disruptions of life in the land caused by the invasions and conquests of the imperial powers – Assyrians, Babylonians, Persians, and later Greeks and Romans. The way of life would remain much the same right down to the present in many rural areas of the Middle East, but the specific feature of the kin-based co-operative may not have survived when the great majority of villages were abandoned under the pressure of war, pestilence and famine between the eighth and the sixth centuries. When the population revived, they were not generally rebuilt in the same places (Faust 2003), and we find a new type of kin-group, the *bet abot* ('fathers' [plural] house), which probably replaced the *mishpaha* (Weinberg 1992: 49–61).

The equality prized in the old Hebrew villages was not the same as any of the kinds of equality we recognize in the modern West. It was really an equality of families or family heads, not of individuals. Within the family, the patriarch had the primacy of honour and could probably enforce his word, and the village was guided by the gathering of such family heads or "elders", as they are called, who also exercised judicial functions (Deut. 21:1–9, 18–21, etc.). Women had an important role within the family, and in work on the land, and mothers expected equal respect with fathers (Exod. 20:12; Lev. 19:3), but they played no part in public life. (See Meyers 1988 for the early period.) Widows and fatherless children had a precarious footing in the social system, which accounts for the frequent injunctions to protect rather than exploiting them.

The concept of honour was of great importance at all levels in ancient society (see Pilch and Malina 1998). The highest positions in society – in a village, the elders – were accorded the greatest honour, while those of no account, such as fatherless children, had little. Women generally had no honour in themselves, but their conduct could confirm or threaten the honour of their menfolk: hence the severe punishment threatened for adultery (sexual relations where the *woman* was married to another man) in the Torah (Lev. 20:10; Deut. 22:22). Honour could be threatened – the man of honour could be shamed – not only by unchaste conduct on the part of his wife or a female relative, but by a failure to fulfil obligations on his own part or on the part of one of his family or supporters, or by a successful challenge to him by a peer or an inferior.

Life in the village was hard. The work was hard, and droughts were frequent. A run of bad years would pose grave threats to life. The growth in population always eventually outran any possible expansion in production. So what happened to the surplus population? And *who* were the surplus population, and who decided it? – a question of justice if ever there was one. We don't know the answers to these questions, but we can make some guesses. First-born sons had an advantage in inheritance (Deut. 21:17), so it seems likely that the further down the birth order a son was, the more likely it was that he would have to leave "to seek his fortune", and the patriarch would determine it (Bendor 1996: 173–90). A daughter would usually have to marry, and would share the fate of the man she had married. A single young man might enlist as a mercenary in foreign service. Desperation led some to banditry, at any rate in the Roman period when economic and political pressures were particularly severe (Horsley and Hanson 1985: 48–87). Probably the most common resort, as today, was to drift to the city, and hope (often in vain) to find work there.

In good years, it is true, the village might enjoy a plentiful surplus, beyond the needs of subsistence, some of which could be exchanged for the few essentials, and even perhaps inessentials, in which the village was not self-sufficient, and the rest stored against the inevitable bad years. (The story of Joseph dramatizes this wisdom on the grand scale.) However, there was no time in our period at which the villages were able to decide for themselves the use of their entire surplus. They existed under the rule of various states which demanded support and imposed taxes, which came directly out of the harvest, and in certain periods conscript military service or forced labour (the "corvée") for the king's building projects (Micah 3:10;

Jer. 22:13; 1 Kgs 12:1–19). There were also the tithes for the support of the clergy. Some, especially in later times, may have paid these gladly as a religious obligation, but they always made it harder to pay secular taxes as well. The village received very little in return for its taxes, and they showed a marked tendency to rise over time. The main reason for this was that the land fell under the rule of the imperial powers, and so there were often two layers of taxes, for the local government and for the empire. The villages under the old monarchies seem to have been able to absorb the impact of taxes with their co-operative ethos, and remain reasonably prosperous (Faust 2000). But the combination of ever-growing taxes, the loss of ancient mechanisms of solidarity, and the neighbourhood of cities containing wealthy men anxious to enrich themselves by lending and to establish themselves as landowners led to farmers more and more frequently falling into debt and being unable to repay.

The impact of debt is sketched very clearly in Neh. 5:1–5. Security (collateral) was always demanded, and failure to repay led to the loss of the security, which might be a family member, who would go into slavery, or a parcel of land. After one or two such crises, the farm would no longer be viable. It would be sold, or seized as security, and the family head would either become a landless labourer, or at best a tenant on the land which had formerly been his family's. Measures of relief as set out in Exod. 21:2–6, Lev. 25:8–17 or Deut. 15:1–2, or applied in Neh. 5:6–11, made no difference in the longer term, if they were applied at all. The picture of rural destitution drawn in Job 24:2–12 suggests the most desperate poverty for the landless poor. The "jubilee" programme offered in Lev. 25:8–55 shows that its author or authors were concerned by the problem of land loss among the rural poor.

Over time, a number of new ways of holding and working the land came into existence alongside the old family freehold, which still survived in NT times (cf. e.g. Lk 15:11–32) (Freyne 1980: 155–207). These included the family farm held as a lease from a landlord who was usually an absentee (Mk 12:1–2), a resident of the city, either for a fixed rent, or on a sharecropping lease. Taxes and tithes still had to be paid, and the chance of retaining any surplus was in either case further reduced. Then there was the estate worked by newly settled tenants (cf. Mk 12:1), who might be discharged soldiers from elsewhere in the empire; and the royal estate, an old institution in Israel (cf. 1 Sam. 8:14), but one which became more extensive under the empires. The estates dominated the more fertile areas and there was a state monopoly in long distance trade, leaving the independent peasants dependent on local markets to sell such surpluses as they were able to keep back from the tax collector.

Villagers became *peasants* in the technical sense of the word, a class working the land in varying degrees of dependence on the upper classes of the cities (Wolf 1966; Lang 1985). They might still be owners of their land, perhaps comfortably off (Lk 15:11–32), but more likely regularly going into debt and having to pay interest, perhaps in a disguised form (Lk 16:5–7; Derrett 1972); they might be tenant farmers or sharecroppers; they might be landless labourers, either working regularly for one master (Mk 1:20), or casually (Mt. 20:1–16); or they might have slipped into slavery (Lk 17:7–10). Although peasants might thus be in very different *economic* circumstances, there is no sign that they saw one another as being of different *social* status. They were united as country people in opposition to the exploiting cities.

At first, they suffered in silence. At most, we hear of protests against the high-handed behaviour of officials and creditors, as in Neh. 5:1–5. However, in the Roman period the ratcheting up of the financial burden on the peasants made people feel they had nothing to lose by rebelling. Agrarian distress is likely to have played a significant part in the repeated rebellions in that period (Horsley and Hanson 1985), though Goodman (2008: 377–418) argues that these were not especially directed against Rome, nor precursors of the great revolt of 66 CE.

The State

As the last few paragraphs will have shown, the leading reason for economic distress in the countryside was the existence of the state and the demands it made on the productivity of the main source of wealth in the country. When we say "the state", we are referring to several different political regimes which exercised power over the area during the period we are concerned with. There were only a few short periods during this long span of time when a native Israelite/Jewish regime exercised sole power. For most of the rest of the time, the area was under an imperial power ruling through governors and collecting taxes for its own use. However, for a very long period Jerusalem had a limited degree of local autonomy under its high priests, who made use of tithes and other offerings. How far its authority extended at any particular time is very uncertain. There were two periods when for most of the time there was a double (or triple) system of government, when local kings controlled internal affairs and raised taxes for their own use but also paid tribute to the current imperial power: the first (c. 740–586 BCE) when kings of Judah (Israel also for a short time) ruled as vassals of the Assyrian king, then after a short break the Egyptian and then the Babylonian king, the second (63 BCE–70 CE) when kings, most of the time Herod and his sons, ruled either the whole or part of the country as clients of the rulers of Rome. All these powers, whether native or foreign, were monarchies (Rome was moving from republican government to *de facto* monarchy in the period up to 31 BCE), though some of them included elements of consultation, for example the council which assisted the high priest, the popular assembly which appears in some of the narratives in Ezra-Nehemiah (Eskenazi 2006), or the Roman Senate, to which the emperor always made a show of deferring. The Roman Senate and emperor were the ultimate rulers also of the cities where Paul exercised his ministry, but they mostly had internal autonomy under a city republican government.

The sources of power for these rulers were several. Consent was an essential factor in all but extreme situations. It was often manufactured by propaganda, and could sometimes be ignored, but power originating in a rebellion such as that of the Maccabees (168 BCE) relied on it to begin with. The other elements were of course force and money. These were bound up together, as the payment of taxes depended on force in the last resort, and soldiers only obeyed if they were paid.

What did the state exist for? There are several ways of answering that question. One way is to state its formal functions. The kings of Israel and Judah were expected to lead the army in battle and thus to protect the realm from its enemies, to grant justice to their subjects, and to oversee the worship of God at the state sanctuaries. The foreign rulers of the land were concerned above all with military security and also exercised judicial power, at least in cases which concerned the security of the state; religious functions could be delegated. The high priests of Jerusalem under those foreign powers therefore had the responsibility of maintaining the proper worship of God, but also of maintaining everyday law and order and settling community disputes.

Another is to say what the state ideally claimed to offer its subjects: later we shall look at the claims of Psalm 72 that the king was favoured by God because of his protection of the poor from exploitation. But third, we might reflect on what the actions of the kings and their agents suggest that they were usually aiming at. Briefly, that is honour, power and wealth, for themselves and possibly for their gods – not for their people, let alone for the abstraction "the nation" which is offered as the concern of modern politicians. For the enormous scale of most regimes' tax demands requires an explanation beyond what was practically required for the discharge of the formal functions of monarchy.

As we have seen, the demands of the original Hebrew monarchs around the eighth century may not have been excessive, and the lack of any royal inscriptions from the time of their rule may be due to more than mere chance: is this the influence of the ethos of simplicity which we have found expressed in their people's villages? But even they used tax revenues for purposes beyond the strictly practical; for example the kings of Israel decorated their palace in Samaria with delicately carved plaques of ivory.

Most subsequent, especially foreign, rulers raised sums horrifying in their impact on what always remained relatively poor economies. The Seleucid kings' rates of land tax at the time of the Maccabean revolt stood at one-third of arable produce and half of the produce of trees (1 Macc. 10:30), and there were other taxes in addition; and many at least of the peasants would also have been paying tithes to the Temple. Such rates are perhaps nothing out of the ordinary for a modern advanced economy; but that is just what the economy of ancient Palestine was not. To lose half one's yearly produce to tax and tithes, with rent perhaps on top of that, probably meant life at the level of mere subsistence. Those who benefited from the taxes, on the other hand, were far fewer, and had opportunity for an enviably comfortable lifestyle.

But that is not the whole of it. Many of the more powerful rulers spent vast sums on public buildings. An impressive example is Herod the Great, who not only rebuilt the temple in Jerusalem on a truly stupendous scale (all that is left today is the lower courses of the western wall, the so-called Wailing Wall, but that is impressive enough), but also palaces of his own, and a pagan temple in Caesarea, which is sufficient indication that his rebuilding of the Jerusalem temple was not due to his excessive devotion to the God of Israel. Naturally all this conspicuous consumption redounded to his glory, and the palaces presumably also ministered to his comfort and his aesthetic sensibility.

Assyrian kings reacted with terrible promptitude to any rebellion of a vassal king. No ordinary Assyrian was harmed by Hezekiah's refusal to "serve" the king of Assyria, that is to pay tribute (2 Kgs 18:7): but the honour of Sennacherib and his god Ashur was insulted, and of course the loss of the tribute was a financial loss. An example had to be shown to other vassals, lest the damage should spread.

There were several ways in which rulers exercised power over their realms. Taxation we have looked at. Obviously troops could be stationed wherever they were required, and fortresses are very common remains of rulers' activity. But they also founded cities, which acted both as power bases where tax officials and soldiers could be based, and as centres of change in the country: thus they could through their economic power reduce the independence of the peasant population, or in the Hellenistic period spread Greek culture among the people. The next section will deal with the society of the cities. Most rulers had crown estates in some parts of the country, and their high officials would also have been given lands in place of a salary (1 Sam. 8:14; Ezek. 46:17), and we have already seen the impact this had on economic relationships in the countryside.

It only remains to observe that there was a standing temptation to misuse the power gathered into the hands of the king and his officials, and there are constant complaints of corruption of justice in the courts and in administration (e.g. for the early period, Isa. 1:23; 5:23; 10:1–2).

The City[1]

We have to distinguish between the native cities of Israel and Judah, of which Jerusalem was the most important survivor into New Testament times, the old Greek cities such as Ephesus, and the new foundations of the Hellenistic kings and the Romans (such as Tiberias or Corinth), which were often colonies in the sense that their populations were imported from elsewhere.

The first type were often built up from villages for strategic or administrative purposes, unless they were old cities surviving or rebuilt from before the Israelite period. Though they were often no bigger than villages, they are distinguished, physically, by the presence of defensive walls and public buildings and a wide range of dwelling sizes, politically, by their selection by the state for military or political purposes, with bureaucratic and military personnel, and socially, by inequality and the stratification of the population into classes (Fritz 1995; Faust 1999b; Faust forthcoming; a more detailed list of characteristics in De Geus 2003: 171). Each city contained a small upper class of high state officials and landowners, and often priests; a large middle class of lower-ranking officials (and priests), craftsmen, tradesmen and so on, as well as usually some farmers; and many poor labourers and outright paupers. Texts such as Isa. 58:7, Ezek. 18:7, Ps. 112:9, testify to the presence of the absolutely destitute. Even the group described as "middle class" by Faust is not likely to have lived much above subsistence level, if one may read back our more extensive

1. See also, in this series, Rogerson and Vincent (2009).

knowledge of cities in Roman and medieval times (cf. Meggitt 1998: 53–59; Friesen 2004: 344). As many of the inhabitants, both rich and poor, would have come into the city from elsewhere, the close-knit family structure of the villages was absent, except in the highest classes, and most of the houses are likely only to have been large enough for a nuclear family (Faust 1999b).

The Hellenistic cities, which were generally larger, also had strategic and administrative functions, but they had a distinctive cultural function too, to cultivate the arts and to be foci of Greek culture in their Semitic environment, sometimes by bringing in settlers from elsewhere in the empire. Obviously there was no such deliberate purpose in the old Greek cities, but there were also Roman colonies in the Greek world, such as Corinth and Philippi. Such cities were more alien to their environment than, say, Jerusalem in Judah. Another important distinction is the far greater importance of commerce in the larger Greek and Hellenistic cities, and the consequent difference in the balance of the population, with more people in various trades, and far more slaves, normally chattel slaves, and freed slaves. The importance of trade may have offered some opportunity in these cities for people (both men and women) to acquire wealth despite their lack of prestige or good birth; Meeks comments on the tensions set up in people who have "status inconsistency", high on some measures of status and low on others (Meeks 1983: 54–55). However, these successful traders would have been much fewer than Meeks seems to allow.

The government of the cities varied. In the old kingdoms it was in the hands of the state officials, who also acted as military commanders and judges; the capitals were under the direct oversight of the king. Judicial procedures were more formal than in the villages (Deut. 19:15–20), but because of the social divisions warnings against favouritism, bribery and class bias were the more necessary (Exod. 23:1–9; Lev. 19:15; Isa. 1:23; 5:23). Cities founded by the Hellenistic kings, such as Tiberias, founded by Herod Antipas (Freyne 1980: 129), or the Romans (e.g. Corinth), as well as old Greek cities, were often technically autonomous ("free cities" in the Roman jargon), and had republican constitutions on the Greek or Roman model. In effect this meant rule by the upper classes, who had the greatest authority and constitutional privileges.

In the cities poor people were more likely to run into financial difficulties and less likely to find help from their families. They could, though, turn to a patron, a better-off or more powerful person who could assist them financially and legally in return for support against his competitors in the struggle for political influence. Patronage, a personal relationship of this sort between a "patron" and a "client", is a central mechanism in the working of many pre-modern societies in which inequality is entrenched, and it is known to be of particular importance in urban society in the Roman period. I have suggested, following R. A. Simkins, that it would also have been important in ancient Israel and Judah (Simkins 1999; Houston 2008: 44–48). In the Old Testament, texts like Lev. 25:35–7 or Deut. 15:7–11 project a relationship of patronage between the addressee and the poor person who is to be helped. It may be said that this is the standard way in which relationships between rich and poor are conceived in the Hebrew Bible, and the main means by which, at least in the cities, resources were shared and channelled.

But unscrupulous patrons could easily be tempted to abuse the relationship. This can be seen clearly in the book of Proverbs, where many sayings urge the reader to be generous to the poor, and almost as many comment that rich people generally do not treat them generously. (These sayings are listed in Houston 2008: 120–21.) One remarks that the poor person who has to borrow ends up as the lender's slave (Prov. 22:7), which may often have been literally true. The usual way in which the independent poor are reduced to dependency in this type of society is by the abuse of credit in the way we have already looked at. It appears to have sometimes been possible for the creditor to seize the debtor him- or herself if the debt was not paid. Hence independent citizens might be sold into permanent slavery, even abroad (Joel 3:6; Neh. 5:8).

The larger cities had a considerable impact on their neighbourhoods and on the village populations there. They needed supplies of food, but this did not necessarily serve as a market incentive for nearby peasant populations, both because of the burden of rents and taxes which made it difficult for them simply to feed themselves, and because of traditional constraints in the way they used the land. However, we find that agriculture in the neighbourhood of large cities does become more intensive, with thickly scattered farmsteads, rather than villages (Faust 2005: 102–03; Carter 1999: 250; Lipschits 2003: 331–32). Many of these will have been created by wealthy inhabitants of the city, who bought land or foreclosed on mortgages to build up estates and establish themselves as landowners (cf. Isa. 5:8; Mic. 2:1–2).

There was much hostility between city and village, because the city was where the landlords and creditors lived, where rents and taxes were gathered and where they were mainly spent, while the city-dwellers looked down on the peasants as ignorant bumpkins – a convenient excuse for ripping them off, and a classic example of ideology. This hostility may be evident in some of the prophetic materials in the Old Testament, but became stronger in the later period, when the cities were culturally alien as well as economically exploitative. It is notable that Jesus is never recorded as having visited the two principal cities of Galilee, Tiberias and Sepphoris, and later on Josephus records the eagerness of the Galilaean peasants to sack them during the great revolt.

The Religious Community

The churches founded by Paul and other missionaries in the Greek cities were not a completely novel form of community. Other societies with a religious object, distinct from the surrounding culture yet not separated from it, had existed or were existing both in the land of Israel and in the Greek cities. In the Old Testament, especially in the stories about Elisha, we hear of the "sons of the prophets" (NRSV "the company of prophets"), who seem to have lived communally together (2 Kgs 6:1–2) under Elisha's leadership. At a later period we find the community who created the Dead Sea Scrolls, the community of Qumran, who not only lived together but had a precise structure and a severe community discipline. Their community documents are among the Dead Sea Scrolls (Vermes 1995). In the Greek cities there were clubs, some of which had a religious purpose, with constitutions and officers, meeting for common meals and for ritual; however, they were not as sharply distinct from the surrounding society as the Christian groups, and a closer parallel would be the Jewish communities in the same cities, who similarly consisted of members that regarded themselves as Philippians, Corinthians and so forth, but whose first loyalty was to Israel, the people of God (Meeks 1983: 31, 77–81).

In the context of the question of justice, it is interesting to decide to what extent the Christian communities reflected the social composition of the cities where they were situated, but their internal relationships are even more important. Both issues are central to the research of Gerd Theissen and Wayne Meeks. There were "not many wise in worldly terms, not many powerful, not many well-born" in the church at Corinth (1 Cor. 1:26); but this was true also of the city of Corinth: as everywhere, the elite were few and the common people many. But it is a question whether there were any genuinely elite or wealthy people at all in the congregation. Theissen and Meeks assert that there was a wide social range among the "first urban Christians", including some who may well have been "powerful" or "well-born", as well as craftspeople, traders and slaves (Theissen 1982: 69–121; Meeks 1983: 51–73). However, this analysis has been sharply challenged more recently. According to Justin Meggitt, none of the evidence used by Theissen and Meeks should be read as pointing to the presence of a wealthy group in the church (Meggitt 1998: 97–154). The houses in which they met need not have been large or those who provided for the church wealthy (ib.: 129–33, 146–48). The Pauline churches "shared fully in the bleak material existence that was the lot of the non-elite inhabitants of the Empire" (Meggitt 1998: 153). Friesen (2004) largely agrees, modifying the picture only slightly to allow for a few individuals with modest surplus resources.

But in any case Meeks recognizes that the relationships of status, power and authority within the congregation are quite different from those without. All the baptized are "brothers" and "sisters", even though some are free and some are slaves – Gal. 3:28. Their status in Christ is more important than their status in the world. However, in practice there are clearly differences of status and relations of authority: but they are different from those in the "world". More women are in responsible and respected positions than in urban society generally. Like other associations, the Christian churches, according to Meeks, depended on patrons, wealthy people who, for example, were able to offer their house for meetings (e.g. 1 Cor. 16:15, 19). Yet these patrons did not control the churches, and Paul notes that the congregations did not defer to them (1 Cor. 16:15), as they certainly would have done to patrons in their life outside the congregation (Meeks 1983: 78). Those who do receive honour are in the first place apostles, such as Paul, who claim authority from a divine commission; and then within the congregation, at least at Corinth, it is clear that those with charismatic gifts have considerable respect and influence.

Meeks suggests that it is status inconsistency in relation to the prominent position of women in the church that is embarrassing Paul when he comes out with the unsatisfactory compromise of 1 Cor. 11:2–16: women may pray and prophesy in the meeting, but they should have their heads covered, in line with social convention, when they do so. The statement later in the same letter (1 Cor. 14:33b–36) that women should not speak at all in the meeting is obviously inconsistent with this, and certainly does not square with his ungrudging recognition of women as fellow workers elsewhere. It may not be an authentic part of the text (Barrett 1968: 332–33).

Challenges to Justice

There are many situations in these social configurations that can be seen as raising challenges to justice, and in most cases the Bible does so. We can categorize them into challenges for the people, for the state and for the individual, which are each seen as capable in different ways of doing justice.

The inclusion here of "the people" may raise the objection that society as such has no decision-making organ, and what happens in society is the outcome of a multitude of practices and decisions by individuals. However, in the Bible itself there is a distinction between texts which impose obligations on the ruler or his agents, or assess their conduct, and ones which call for social action without naming a responsible person – an obvious example of the latter is the "jubilee" legislation in Leviticus 25. And there is a clear political reason for this. Much of the Bible was written at a time when Judaism formed some kind of polity, but lacked the authority of the state, which was held by the imperial power. It is unlikely that the high priest could have enforced the jubilee decrees of Lev. 25:8–17 even if he had wanted to. On the other hand, the sabbatical commands of Lev. 25:1–7 and Deut. 15:1–2 were widely observed in Second Temple Judah, as we know from Josephus and from the Mishnah, the collection of Jewish law made around 200 CE (M. *Sheb.* 10). The one was a matter of ancient custom (cf. Exod. 23:10–11), and the other was a sensible corollary: the repayment of debts should not be enforced when no produce was being brought in. (But it may well have meant more than that: see Chirichigno 1993: 272–75 and Houston 2008: 181–82.) I therefore make a distinction between challenges to society at various levels, some of which could have been met by the state or local polity, and challenges to the ruler.

Within the society of the village, issues of justice arose in the treatment of the weaker members of the *bet ab*, the younger sons, the widows and the fatherless. As we have seen, the question was who were to enjoy the fruits of what in the early period was a modestly prosperous economy, and who were to be forced out to take their chances in the city, or, as taxes and other financial pressures mounted, to be handed over to the creditors as debt slaves. To put it another way, were the principles of equality that Israelite people valued to be applied within the *bet ab* as well as between one *bet ab* and another? In fact, the questions raised in this paragraph receive relatively little attention in the Bible, probably because of its largely urban origin.

Within the city, we are dealing at all times with a society that is internally vastly more unequal than the village, and becomes increasingly exploitative of the countryside also as time goes on. The issues include the question of debt, or rather of credit and its abuse; slavery, which was the result either of debt or of war; the corrupt administration of justice; the welfare of the destitute; and the fundamental issue of inequality in itself, which is plainly the root of all the other problems. We shall find that the Bible confronts most of these issues in one way or another. But despite the egalitarian heritage of Israel, most OT writers take the existence of rich and poor for granted, and exhort the rich to be generous to the poor, or denounce them for exploiting them, rather than addressing the structure of society to eliminate the imbalance of power. A more radical approach emerges in parts of the New Testament, but this also has no sense of social structure: it is a vision of a simple reversal of relationships.

Within the early Christian communities the question was whether they were going to treat each other as equals in Christ, despise those whose charismatic qualifications were not as good as others', or retain values of city society in the way they treated each other. We should not know about these problems if Paul had not compelled them to confront them.

But the deep cleavage between city and country, which became deeper as time went on, and the problem of class division within each city, were themselves only symptoms of the more fundamental inequity of society as a whole, in which the ruling class, native and foreign, cornered by way of taxes, tithes and rents ultimately a good half of the wealth of the country (cf. Lenski 1966: 228–29), though probably less in the old kingdoms, and left the original producers of that wealth little more than what they needed to stay alive. It will therefore be important to see to what extent this issue is addressed in the Bible. The utopian social visions of Leviticus and Deuteronomy only address it by implication: such ruinous exploitation is simply absent.

It might therefore be thought that the state would be seen more as the fount of injustice than of justice; and indeed this is normally true of the imperial powers (Babylon eventually comes to stand for them all). But despite wariness in some texts about monarchy, the Davidic monarchy is again and again seen as the proper source of justice. It was so successful in presenting itself as the defender of the poor from oppression that the title "Messiah" (or king) came to be thought appropriate for a radical assailant of privilege, and the rule of king Messiah in some circles the only acceptable constitution for the eschatological people of God (Horsley and Henson 1985: 110–34). This development was of course aided by the fact that the Davidic monarchy no longer existed, and at a time of deepening exploitation by foreign powers the myth of the righteous king could shape both the past and the future.

The one role of the individual, other than the king, which is constantly addressed is that of patron. A righteous man (always so gendered), according to the various definitions offered in the Old Testament, is one who is generous to the poor and does not oppress them (e.g. Ps. 112:9; Houston

2008: 99–131). But it is clear from some texts that the solidarity so demanded can only be realized within the community of those who are in principle equals, neighbours, "brothers", to use the gendered language of Deuteronomy, even though this is not really compatible with the patron-client relationship (let alone the master-slave relationship which it sometimes becomes). Therefore in the end the individual can only be just if the society in which he or she lives is just.

Chapter 3

THE STORY OF CREATION: JUSTICE AS COSMIC ORDER

Narratives of Justice

All the overarching narratives of justice which the Bible tells in response to the challenges we have identified are in one way or another stories about God. It is the just God who is finally responsible for the justice of humanity. But like all theologies, the theology of the Bible can only conceive of God in human terms. The justice of God is conceived on the pattern of human justice: which, as God is understood as a powerful individual, means either the justice of the king, or the justice of the patron. The presentation of God as king is of course prominent in many places in the Bible, and is recognized by everyone. But it has not been understood until recently that in other places in the Old Testament it is helpful to envisage the action of YHWH in relation to Israel as that of a patron (cf. Houston 2008: 204–26). It may prove possible to extend this understanding into the New Testament.

This means that we should be able to bring much of what the Bible says about justice into two broad narratives. The first (this chapter) is the story of the king who impartially establishes justice in his kingdom. In the ideology of ancient near eastern kingdoms the king is always understood to do this as the agent of the divine. Justice in the social realm is understood as a reflex of the order in the cosmic realm which is established at creation. At the same time we shall need to recognize that this *is* ideology: although, in the human sphere, it does correspond to *some* genuine royal activity for justice, its main function is to obscure the *in*justice and *dis*order created by the greed of the state. But then again, God's kingly justice is in the Bible seen as a reality, which ends by destroying the oppressive state and establishing human life anew in justice: the fall of Babylon and the new Jerusalem.

The second story (Chapter 4) is that of the patron who successfully defends his client from oppression. The pattern story is of course the exodus, YHWH's deliverance of Israel from Egypt, which is cited repeatedly in

Exodus and Deuteronomy as the model for human patrons' behaviour towards their clients. This is often taken as *the* narrative of God's justice in the Bible. Yet, although in relation to Pharaoh YHWH does act as a king deals with a rebellious vassal (Brueggemann 1995), in relation to Israel YHWH's commitment creates many incidental acts of injustice to others, and must be understood as the *partial*, biased justice of a patron (Houston 2006: 206–09; 2007). It is this partial, one-to-one relationship which is expressed in the various narratives of covenants in the Pentateuch and elsewhere, and this is again how YHWH's justice is understood in Isaiah 40–55. I think it can be shown that Paul's understanding of the righteousness of God is in the same line. God's justice is revealed by justifying those who put their faith in Christ, who are thereby within God's covenant.

These two ideas of justice stand in tension with each other, but they are *both* essential in the biblical understanding to a rounded picture of divine justice; and much of what is said in the Bible about human justice can be drawn under these heads, but not all. Justice, as we have seen, can and must be done by the people as a body, not just by kings and patrons, and the ideal structure of the covenant people is understood as one of equality – harking back to a deeply embedded feature of Israelite rural culture. Chapter 5 will be concerned with texts emphasizing this understanding. Again, the theme carries through into the New Testament and the correspondence of Paul with his churches.

Although Jesus the Christ is seen as Messiah, "son of David", the final representative of the Davidic monarchy, the way in which he expresses his Messiahship is so radically new that it would be misleading simply to class his ministry as one expression of the kingly justice dealt with in this chapter. The reversal of expectations is seen not only in the reversal of destiny in the beatitudes as given in Lk 6:20–23, a characteristic apocalyptic theme, but more radically in "the Son of Man who came not to be served but to serve, and to give his life a ransom for many", presented in Mark (10:45) as the pattern for the disciples in their relationships with each other. This will be our theme in Chapter 6.

Justice as Order in Creation

The leading feature of the creation of the world in many parts of the Old Testament, as in such narratives in related ancient cultures, is the establishment of order over against chaos. This is manifestly the case on the first page of the Bible, in Gen. 1:1–2:3, where creation begins with God making a series of "divisions" in the previously undifferentiated mass of "darkness over the face of the deep" (1:2): light from darkness, the water above the firmament from the water below, the dry land from the sea. This ordering process involves time as well as space: day is distinguished from night, each day of creation is marked, and the seventh day, on which God rests from his work, is blessed and consecrated. This ordered framework of space and time ("heaven and earth", 1:1; 2:1) enables plant, animal and human life to flourish (to "be fruitful and multiply") within it.

But it is not immediately obvious in this best-known narrative of creation that the order established at creation is one of justice. It is other narratives, and particularly those of a more poetic character, as in the Psalms, that bring this out. I should like to start with the great song of praise with which Psalm 89 begins. The theme of the Psalm is expressed in the first four verses: the faithful commitment of YHWH to his[1] chosen one, David and his house after him. In the last part of the Psalm (vv. 38–51[2]), it will ask in the light of the disaster which has overtaken the house whether that faithfulness was not an illusion. But vv. 5–14 celebrate the greatness of YHWH and his work in creation, before going on to concentrate on his goodness to his people and to his king. It is important to notice that the poet's attention here covers YHWH himself and his foundation of the world, but it is not a celebration of the past act of creation for its own sake. The purpose of mentioning events of the past is for their secure foundation of the world that now exists. This is true of creation doctrine in the ancient Near East in general. Verses 9–10 tell of YHWH's defeat of his mythical enemies, including the raging sea that threatens the world. Verse 11 takes in the entire universe as then understood, and affirms that it (now and always) belongs to YHWH because YHWH created it.

The key verse for us is v. 14. It is the climax of the description of YHWH in himself before the subject changes to the people in their relation to YHWH. "Righteousness and justice (*tsedeq umishpat*) are the foundation of your throne, loyal love and faithfulness (*hesed we'emet*) are your advance guard." These two pairs of attributes are essential to every conception of

1. While I have attempted to avoid the use of the masculine pronoun in reference to God where the context is belief at the present day or in general, the sensitive reader need not be sheltered from the gendered character of Hebrew speech about God in the Old Testament – and should not, if it is to be honestly assessed.

2. Verse references are to the English Bible. Verse 52 is not part of the Psalm, but the doxology which concludes Book III of the Psalter.

right relationships, both divine and human, in the Hebrew Bible. They frequently go together, but their connotations are different. *Tsedeq* ("right", "right dealings") and *mishpat* ("justice") have to do with the way one treats those that one has dealings with, and with the right order of society as a whole. *Hesed* ("loyal love", "steadfast love"), and *'emet* ("truth", "faithfulness") have to do with a person's generosity in helping the particular person or group he or she is committed to, and their firmness in that commitment. They recur again and again in this Psalm in connection with YHWH's covenant with David (vv. 25, 28, 33, 49), and it is appropriate that they should be mentioned at this point, just as the text turns its attention to the people. But the immediate context is the universal, cosmic power and action of God. In this context the "right dealing" and "justice" of YHWH come first. They imply that the way YHWH has ordered the universe is right and just.

What does this actually mean? Psalm 89 at this point begins to focus on the particular relationship of YHWH with his people and especially with his anointed. We shall return to this in a moment. A sharper focus on the meaning of justice in the order of the cosmos is provided by Psalm 82, a unique little psalm, in which God (YHWH, here called Elohim) announces a verdict on the (other) gods, who seem to be presented as real but failing beings. (The more advanced conception in, e.g., Ps. 96:5 considers these gods nothing but idols.) Since they are the gods of other nations, the implication is that they have been entrusted with the celestial government of those nations. This is explicit in Deut. 32:8–9 as it is translated in NRSV, following the Greek version: "the Most High ... fixed the boundaries of the peoples according to the number of the gods". God accuses them: "How long will you judge corruptly and show favouritism to the wicked? Vindicate the poor and the orphan, give judgment in favour of the wretched and the poor. Deliver the poor and the needy, and rescue them from the power of the wicked' (Ps. 82:2–4). From this it appears that an important role of a god is to ensure just relationships in human society by protecting the poor and repressing exploitation. These so-called gods have failed to do this, and are condemned to die, although supposedly immortal. The poet concludes (v. 8) by calling on God himself, in his justice, to take over the gods' role for "all the nations". A "right and just" cosmos is one where, among other things, human society is "right and just", and that means one where the poor come first.

Thus the affirmation in Ps. 89:14 that "right and justice" are the foundation of God's throne is an affirmation that God orders the whole cosmos in justice, and human society as part of the cosmos. It is for this reason that in Psalms 96 and 98, when the "coming" of YHWH to "judge" the earth is celebrated, the whole of nature is called on to rejoice (Ps. 96:11–13; 98:7–9). These psalms, along with the other so-called "psalms of enthronement" in Psalms 93, 96–99, celebrate YHWH's kingship. This implies his rule in the first place over other gods (Ps. 95:3; 96:4; 97:7), then over the hostile forces of chaos (Ps. 93:3–4; 29:3, 10; 89:9–10), over his own creation (95:4–5; 96:11–13; 97:4–5; 98:7–9), and over all nations (96:10; 99:2–3), but especially over his own people (95:7; 97:8; 98:3; 99:4–8). This motif of divine kingship, as well as that of cosmic justice, is exemplified in comparable material from other ancient Near Eastern cultures. It is associated with God's foundation of the world (Ps. 93:1–2; 96:10), but also with his continuing maintenance of a just order, and this is what is meant by his "coming to judge". No distinction is made between God's judgement of the peoples and of the earth or the world: nature and society are equally under the divine rule. And the object of "judging" is to restore justice where it has been damaged.

For the Old Testament testifies to a profound breach in the just order of creation, for which creatures themselves are responsible. Let us return to the first creation narrative, with which we began. At the end of the sixth day, after the creation of human beings, God speaks to them and grants them the seeds of plants and the fruit of trees as their food; and to the animals he grants the green stuff of the plants (Gen. 1:29–30). He says nothing about animal food for either. This is not how things are today, when many animals prey on other animals, and human beings also eat animal food. Later, after the Flood, he permits people to eat meat, and implies that animals also will act aggressively (9:2–6). What has happened in the meantime? What has happened is that God's just and well-ordered creation has been wrecked by being filled with *violence*, and every living thing ("all flesh") has made a wreckage of its conduct (6:11–13). "Violence" represents the Hebrew *hamas*, which has been defined as "criminal oppression of the unprotected by those mightier than they" (Gunkel 1997: 143). In other words, it is the opposite of justice. This is the reason that God gives for bringing the flood; yet the flood is unable to mend things. That is how things stay. The injustice between creatures is not God's intention in creation; but it is held in check, violently, by human beings (9:3). (Rogerson (1991: 18–25) discusses a number of readings of Genesis 1–9 along these lines. See also Fretheim 2005: 80–84; and Houston forthcoming.)

So in the view of the priestly writer in Genesis it would be possible to speak of justice and injustice (even if he does not use those words) in the relations between all creatures, not just between human beings. Today we must be conscious of how overwhelming is the injustice and violence used by us human beings, armed with our science and technology, against the earth and all its creatures. It puts relationships on quite a different footing from anything that the Hebrew writers would have recognized; yet we can still learn from their moral evaluation of the life of God's creatures.

The Just King

Returning to Psalm 89, that psalm sets alongside the praise of YHWH as king of the cosmos his appointment of a human king to be his deputy on earth, to whom YHWH commits his faithful support in covenant (vv. 28–37). Along with other "royal psalms", this psalm presents David and his heirs as in principle kings of the whole earth (vv. 25, 27; cf., e.g., Ps. 2:8–11; 18:43; 72:8–11), despite the fact that their actual realm was a small impoverished mountain principality. This is an indication that the motif was an essential part of the internationally shared royal ideology. The deputy of the world's ruler must be a world ruler! Like YHWH, David will, with YHWH's help, destroy his enemies (Ps. 89:22–23; cf. 2:9; Psalms 18; 20; 21, etc.), for they are YHWH's enemies. Like YHWH, David is to rule in justice (Ps. 18:20–24; 45:4; 72:1–4, 12–14; 101), for his justice is YHWH's (Ps. 72:1). In the order of being, as the ancient theologian understands it, David's kingship is derived from YHWH's. In the order of knowledge, YHWH's kingship is understood through that of David. In the order of ideology, YHWH's kingship is modelled on David and is the warrant for David's; his power is justified because he is YHWH's agent.

Psalm 72 is the best of all the royal psalms to demonstrate the working of this ideology in detail, and is the one psalm that foregrounds the king's justice (Houston 1999 and 2008: 139–50). The gift which the poet asks for for the king is God's "justice" and "right" (*tsedaqa*); the latter appears again in v. 3. This combination elsewhere tends to refer to what we mean by "social justice", and from the start this is the emphasis here: vv. 2, 4 and 12–14 make clear that it is to be the king's task to deliver the poor from oppression. But *tsedaqa* has a wider sense, as it often does: "May the mountains yield prosperity for the people, and the hills, *in right*" (v. 3; cf. v. 7). This is God's cosmic rule of right which brings fertility and peace and prosperity, as in vv. 6–7, 16. If the king rules according to God's justice and right, this is what will happen in his realm. It is not the result of his adopting sensible economic policies, but of his ruling in "righteousness".

The prayer continues with petitions for the king's universal rule (vv. 8–11); and then takes a distinctive turn: "*For* he delivers the needy person when he calls ..." (vv. 12–14). I have argued that this "For" implies that the prayer for his rule over the nations is justified by the king's concern and activity for the poor (Houston 2008: 142). This implies in turn that the legitimacy of the king's rule rests on this activity for social justice, and thus that the prosperity which the prayer also asks for is likewise dependent on the king's justice. This responsibility of protecting the poor from oppression is, as we have seen, a central aspect of the justice of God, and similar language to that used of the king is used of God in, e.g., Ps. 12:5; 18:27; 35:10 ("saving" the poor); 69:18 ("redeem my life"); 116:15 ("precious in the sight of YHWH is the death of his faithful ones").

These verses appear to offer the king's concern and action for the poor to God as a fact, which makes it proper to ask for the blessings that the psalm does ask for (Houston 2008: 140, with n. 20). The obvious question is whether it really was a fact, or simply an aspiration, or merely propaganda. There is decidedly little evidence for it: a verse in 1 Samuel (8:15) about David, which hardly counts as historical evidence; Jeremiah's praise of Josiah (Jer. 22:15–16), which may be over-enthusiastic; and the story of the liberation of Hebrew slaves in Jerusalem under covenant in the reign of Zedekiah (Jer. 34:8–11), at the very end of the Davidic monarchy, and rapidly undone. Nevertheless, as I have maintained (Houston 1999: 357–59; 2008: 147), the kings would have had an interest in cutting powerful figures in society down to size, and a popular way of doing it would be to accuse them of exploitation of the poor. Thus they would have had an interest in acting to protect the poor, and could have done so by judicial means, responding to petitions and appeals, by administrative means, issuing decrees remitting debts and taxes, as kings in other states are known to have done, and in the last resort by force (see Weinfeld 1995).

But if this is true, the psalm conceals the fact that if the king was active on behalf of the poor, it was his self-interest rather than his concern which motivated him. Even more seriously, it conceals the exploitative activity of the monarchy, which raised taxes from the farming population for largely unproductive purposes. It is a prime specimen of ideology. It is a successful example of ideology because it responds to a widespread popular conviction that looking after the poor is what kings ought to do. This conviction goes back to the third millennium BCE in Mesopotamia, and in the Old Testament it is the test of the king's justice both in texts like this one that are supportive of the monarchy (see also Prov. 31:8–9) and in some that are critical or suspicious of it: see, for example, Jer. 22:3, 15–16; 23:5; Ezekiel 34.

I have suggested that we should not simply read ideological texts like this as propaganda, concealing facts, falsifying reality and misdirecting their readers. We should read them as challenging and even changing reality, forcing the powerful who patronize their writing to apply them to themselves, or if they do not, entitling the readers to challenge the legitimacy of their rule. So you are entitled to rule the world because you are good to the poor? Well, be good to the poor, then! This Psalm in particular undermines the version of the "divine right of kings" which is suggested in Psalm 89 and other royal psalms, where YHWH makes an absolute promise to maintain the dynasty even if they do wrong (Ps. 89:30–33). It is still true in Psalm 72 as in Psalm 89 that the king's right to rule is derived from God. But whereas in Psalm 89 this rests on God's arbitrary choice (vv. 19–20), in Psalm 72 it rests on the king's fulfilment of God's charge of justice. Some Christian political thinkers, as long ago as the Middle Ages, derived from this a right of rebellion against unjust rulers (O'Donovan and O'Donovan 1999: e.g. 281–82, 695–701), and all may take from it the conviction that authority is only valid when it takes the protection of the weakest in society as its first duty. John Rawls, the American author of one of the leading modern theories of justice, argues that inequalities are justified only to the extent that the least well-off are benefited as a result (Rawls 2001: 42–43, 61–66); may one trace here in a secular philosopher the enduring influence of the Bible in a Christian culture?

It is important to note that this conception of political legitimacy is not only quite different from the ancient idea of the divine right of kings, but also from the liberal-democratic doctrine that authority should rest on the choice of the people. Christians of all people should have the courage to say that the people can be wrong, and can choose evil rulers. There is a contradiction in democracy when it is interpreted as it is in the modern liberal state as the opportunity for people to pursue their own interests politically within a capitalist economic system: society becomes a collective of competing interests with increasing inequality rather than a community of equals. "Democracy has won its global near-monopoly as basis for legitimate rule in a setting which largely contradicts its own pretensions" (Dunn 2005: 187; see the whole chapter, 149–88).

At the same time, we need to recognize that the notion of justice in this psalm has its own serious drawbacks (Houston 2008: 149–50). It means essentially the redress of grievances. It is limited to repairing the inroads made by the powerful on the rights of the weak, and does not envisage any change in the system which enables such assaults to be made. Moreover, it is a top-down sort of justice. The king decides when justice has been breached, and how the breach is to be repaired and the poor delivered. There is no sense that the poor might take the initiative in their own defence, and become "subjects of their own history", to use a phrase from the liberation theologians. For such an idea of justice, we must look to another narrative.

Nevertheless, for all its drawbacks, and self-interested as it might be in its origins, the narrative of royal justice became the template for many an evocation of the good society in the centuries after the fall of the Davidic dynasty. All four of the main collections of prophetic material in the Old Testament contain "Messianic" visions or prophecies. One of the most striking is Isa. 11:1–9. The first part, vv. 1–5, emphasizes the future king's justice, and as in Psalm 72 it is above all justice for the poor: "he shall give right judgment for the poor, and pronounce with equity for the wretched of the land" (v. 4 – not the NRSV's "the meek of the earth" in this context!). The really interesting part is in the continuation in vv. 6–9, the famous vision of the "peaceable kingdom" in which wolf and lamb, leopard and kid, live peacefully side by side, and the predators are converted into harmless herbivores.

Like any thoroughly pictorial poetry, this is open to a range of interpretation. We have already seen that there is a strand in the thinking of the Hebrew Bible which regards the fact that animals prey on each other as a corruption of God's original intention in creation. The ideal of peaceful relationships between the creatures, like other ideals, can be presented either as the original perfection, from which the world has declined, or as the consummation it will reach in the ultimate future, as a result of the rule of the Messianic king. However, in the context this perhaps traditional eschatological expectation seems to be being used as a metaphorical picture of a human society in which exploitation has been done away with, through a transformation or conversion of people rather than through the coercive power of the shoot of Jesse. The whole passage is bound together by referring to the "knowledge of YHWH" at the beginning (v. 2) and the end (v. 9). At the beginning it is a supernatural endowment of the messianic king; at the end it is universal, as common as water is in the sea. "The divine education in justice needs to be appropriated by all, not just a responsible elite" (Houston 2008: 156).

We have here moved a long way beyond the top-down justice of the royal ideology. We move beyond it in a different way in the Gospels, but still without losing sight of the basic insight of Psalm 72. Jesus is proclaimed son of God – that is, Messiah – by the voice from heaven at his baptism (Mt. 3:17; Mk 1:11; Lk 3:22), which alludes strongly to Ps. 2:7 and also to

Isa. 42:7, so drawing on the royal ideology. But when he himself addresses the subject of political power (brought up by the sons of Zebedee), he transforms expectations by the paradoxical teaching that one who wishes to rule must be "the slave of all", and interprets his own ministry along the same lines: he has come both to serve and to give his life for all (Mk 10:44–5). "Precious is their blood ..." – precious enough to give his own. Such, at least, is Mark's insight into its meaning. We shall come back to this in Chapter 6.

God's Vindication of Cosmic Justice in the Wisdom Literature

Leaving the royal and messianic action for justice, we return to consider God's own justice in other contexts.

One of the most widespread ways in the Bible of conceiving the maintenance or restoration of cosmic justice is the connection asserted between act and consequence. When one does good, the good consequences, the blessing that results, will return to one; when one does evil, the evil consequences likewise will eventually strike one.

Many of the sayings in Proverbs are specifically concerned with the issue of social justice, and warn of the fate awaiting those who exploit the poor: see 14:31; 17:5; 21:13; 22:16; 22:22–23; 23:10–11; 28:8. Far more simply speak of the "righteous" (or just) and the "wicked" (or unjust), but José Miranda argues that these words should always be interpreted specifically of the way people treat the poor (Miranda 1977: *passim*). In fact there is a saying in Proverbs (29:7) which would justify this: "A just man (*tsaddiq*) knows the rights of the poor, but an unjust man (*rasha*) has no insight."

The issue of social justice is likewise central to the book of Job (Brueggemann 1994; Pleins 2001: 504–10). The one-sentence pronouncements of Proverbs are developed into full narratives in the speeches of Job's friends. Zophar's second speech in Job 20 is one of the best examples: it presents the story of a wicked man[3] who amasses riches by oppressing the poor, and ends by being forced to disgorge them. "He swallowed down riches and vomited them up again; God turned them out of his belly" (Job 20:15). Carol Newsom sees narratives like this as making a claim about fundamental reality, the cosmic order of justice, as I would call it, and argues that they are convincing because they "encode fundamental commitments, social roles and profiles of virtue that constitute the

---

3. Except for one word in v. 5, the Hebrew has the masculine singular. The NRSV's plural weakens the force of the Hebrew.

community". They make sense to one who tries to live a virtuous life in the kind of society that they presuppose, "a hierarchical, paternalistic social order based on kinship and something like a patronage system" (Newsom 2003: 122–23). In other words, they are ideological, and like other ideologies may be seen, as I have argued, as not merely making sense in a particular kind of society, but also serving to defend it in the face of experiences of injustice (Houston 2008: 124–26). The oppressed are assured that in the long run their oppressors will be forced to disgorge their ill-gotten gains and end their lives in misery. Because the cosmic order is just, the social order cannot be unjust for long. The book of Job exposes the unreliability of such stories, but this does not stop people believing them, and continuing to tell them.

Often in the wisdom literature cosmic justice seems to be presented as an automatic connection which does not require any divine intervention; e.g. each of the four sayings in Prov. 11:3–6 seem to say that the righteousness of the righteous or the wickedness of the wicked is the direct cause of their fate. However, Proverbs sometimes refers to YHWH as the direct agent of reward or retribution, e.g. 15:25, 29 or 19:17, which asserts that YHWH will reward one who is generous to a poor man; and conversely we sometimes find the prophets presenting natural disaster as the automatic consequence of evil in the social realm (e.g., Hos. 4:1–3).

God's Vindication of Cosmic Justice in the Prophets

However, in the historical books and the prophets YHWH is regularly affirmed to be the agent of retribution. The books of Judges and Kings assert that Israel's fate depended on their loyalty or disloyalty to YHWH. The prophets proclaim a word of judgement in the name of YHWH, who personally announces his sentence on evildoers. YHWH's watch over injustice is not confined to his people Israel. The book of Amos opens with a series of pronouncements of judgement on all of Israel's neighbours, mostly for what we would call war crimes: massacres, brutality, disrespect to the dead, selling whole peoples into slavery. Only then does the finger point to the social injustice going on in the cities of Israel.

The mechanism of retribution for the human crimes of injustice and brutality may be human, in the form of war, invasion, subjugation and deportation (constantly in the prophets), or it may be natural: a whole range of natural disasters are presented as YHWH's acts of judgement in Amos 4:6–11, and of these earthquake (v. 11) is mentioned several times again (8:8; 9:1, 5–6), and the dating of Amos's words "two years before the earthquake" (1:1) suggests that the editors of Amos thought the massive earthquake in the mid-eighth century BCE mentioned in Zech. 14:5 was, to some extent, their fulfilment. This shows how YHWH's justice is understood as exercised in the world as a whole, with no distinction between the natural and the human realms. Many prophetic oracles announce what we sometimes call "poetic justice", in which the punishment symbolically fits the crime, for example Isa. 3:11; in Isa. 5:8–10 the punishment for landgrabbers is to find that the land they have seized is infertile, producing a fraction of the amount of seed sown. This is not just "poetic": it makes sense in a view of the world in which nature and society are a seamless whole, and action in the social world produces consequences in the natural world (Marlow 2009: 120–243).

It would follow that at least some of the sins condemned in the prophets should be seen as violations of the natural order of justice maintained by YHWH. The case has been made incisively in a valuable paper by John Barton (Barton 1979 = 2003: 32–44). But this is controversial. Some argue that the prophets are ministers of the covenant, and condemn Israel for disobedience to YHWH their God's express commands (e.g. Sloane 2008: 76). This is true to a limited extent: Ezekiel, and to some extent Jeremiah, do take this line. But such things as covenants and commandments are not part of the discourse of earlier prophets, apart from a couple of references to a covenant in Hosea. As Miranda points out, one might have expected them to have least occasionally quoted a law if their complaint was that Israel had broken God's laws (Miranda 1977: 166). But they do not. And we have already seen that foreign nations, who do not know YHWH's express commands, are also condemned. Rather, when Amos asks that "justice should flow like water, and right like a never-failing stream" (Amos 5:24), he is asking that Israel's life should conform to the justice and right which are the foundation of YHWH's throne, and on the basis of which he has created the world. Whether or not this moral standard is thought to be revealed at Sinai, its basis is in creation. This does not mean in either case that their hearers could be expected to *know* it "naturally" – Jer. 5:4–5 implies that some might have better opportunities to learn than others; but know it they should. They would have been taught them by their parents and by elders in the community; in places it is particularly the function of the priests (Hos. 4:4–6; Jer. 18:18). If they do not act accordingly, it may be because they do *not* know (see, e.g. Isa. 1:3, 5:13, Hos. 4:6), but that is no excuse.

The content of this natural justice is much the same for every prophet, but its application varies somewhat according to the issues uppermost for each. People should treat each other with honesty, generosity and respect rather than with dishonesty, grasping and meanness, cruelty, violence and disrespect. Clearly this is a message which needs to be heard above all by the strong in respect of their conduct towards those who are weaker than they. The central issue for Amos is the exploitation of the poor by those on whom they are forced to depend for employment, for loans or for food; and the failure of the courts to do anything about it (Amos 5:10, 15). For Micah, who does not refer to the victims of oppression as "poor", the main issues are the seizure of agricultural land (Mic. 2:1–2), the ruthless use of conscript labour by the authorities (3.1–3, 9–10), and the corruption of political and religious authority and commercial integrity by greed and dishonesty (3:5, 11; 6:10–12).

In Isaiah most of these are issues; but John Barton may well be right in seeing Isaiah's ethics as based on a hierarchical ideal of the world (society *and* cosmos), as implied in 3:1–7, under the ultimate supremacy of YHWH as God (Barton 1980 = 2003: 130–44). In 5:16 YHWH is exalted and his holiness asserted, and this *is* "justice and right". His self-assertion as supreme is prophesied in Isa. 2:9–22. "Justice and right" under this definition would include deference to superiors; the inversion of this value is prophesied as an unwelcome fate in 3:12, and 3:1–8 threatens Jerusalem and Judah with the collapse of a well-ordered hierarchy as the consequence (poetic justice again!) of their rebellion against the supremacy of YHWH. But justice must equally include care and concern for the humble, whom instead the "elders and officials of his people" grind down and exploit (3:13–15). The converse of "justice and right" in Jerusalem in 1:21–23 is miscarriage of justice resulting from judicial corruption; in 5:7 it is bloodshed and bitter complaint. YHWH's exaltation in justice and right in 5:16 is the flipside of the destruction of Jerusalem and the exile of its people, and this results in peaceful grazing in the ruins for the "lambs and kids", a transparent veil for the humble ones of YHWH's people.

The prophets who foreground Israel's *religious* disloyalty to YHWH, above all Hosea, Jeremiah and Ezekiel, are not in disagreement with Amos, Micah and Isaiah. But the narrative of justice that they are working with is the one dealt with in the next chapter, the story of YHWH's saving commitment to one human partner, the people of Israel, demanding an answering exclusive commitment in return, rather than the rule of the one creator God in justice over the whole earth.

In the meantime, you may object that this account of the prophets makes them, especially Isaiah, conservative supporters of the established order, rather than radically subverting it, as they have normally been presented. What kind of justice is this? My answer is that it is indeed a conservative kind of justice. The prophets maintained the theological and ethical traditions of their people, which required in YHWH's name fair and honest and respectful treatment for all, even if a higher order of respect was asked for the elders and other leaders than for others. Effective social critics, as Michael Walzer argues, derive their critique from the traditions of their people (Walzer 1987). It was the governments and their urban supporters that were sitting light to those traditions as they set about transforming the social order for the sake of their power, their wealth and their glory, building cities, raising armies, squeezing out taxes. The prophetic books came to be composed after those regimes had fallen, using as a basis whatever the prophets' supporters had preserved or could remember of their words, in order to show that they fell because of their failure to live in justice and right as YHWH required, both as a way of dealing with the theological problem of the disaster and as a warning for the future.

Of course, those rulers claimed to live and to rule by the same standards, as we have seen. The prophets did not disagree with the urban governing class about morality in the abstract. As literate intellectuals they were members of the same class, and you will not find the authentic words of the exploited poor themselves in their books. Nor did they undertake any structural criticism of the social situation as might be done today; they had not got the tools for that. Where they differed from others of their class was in having the impudence to take their moral standards seriously and apply them to their conduct rather than their aspirations.

The prophetic tradition of divine justice is carried forward into the New Testament. Jesus appears in the Synoptic Gospels as the preacher of the kingdom of God. The connection of this idea with Old Testament presentations of God as king and "judge of all the earth" is obvious. In the Psalms, the expectation of God's coming in judgement may well have its setting in the annual festival of Tabernacles, and may represent a conviction that God sets the world to rights annually. This expectation had been sharpened in the meantime by the development of the apocalyptic conviction that this world was in the grip of Satan (cf. e.g. Mt. 12:25–9; Lk 11:17–22, which parallel God's kingdom with Satan's). There can be little doubt this was encouraged by the rule of foreign empires with their ruthless demands. In Luke's presentation of Jesus' ministry, he uses Isa. 61:1–2 as his programme (Lk 4:18–21), which is essentially an announcement of the restoration of cosmic justice in the setting of Second Temple Judaism: note especially the leading place taken by "announcing good news to the poor".

Two chapters later, Jesus' teaching ministry is formally launched with the pronouncement of the beatitudes and woes (Lk 6:20–26): four precisely matched antithetical pairs of sayings which function as prophecies of a total reversal in the material state of classes in society. The initial terms in each series, the poor and the rich, evidently embrace the following two in each case – the case of being expelled and insulted or else spoken well of is somewhat different. The opening blessing of the poor, "for yours is the kingdom of God", says all that needs to be said about the way in which Jesus' teaching stands in the prophetic tradition. But he does not say the same thing as the Old Testament prophets! As we shall see shortly, there is a weakness in most judgement prophecy in the Old Testament in that it tends to involve the victims of oppression in the same fate as their oppressors. This the beatitudes and woes avoid, by deliberately contrasting their fate. Similar contrasts emerge in other teaching in the Synoptic Gospels, for example the picture of the judgement of the nations ("parable of the sheep and the goats") in Mt. 25:31–46, or the parable of the rich man and Lazarus in Lk 16:19–31. In Mk 10:24–25 Jesus emphasizes how difficult it will be for the rich to enter the kingdom of God. In the kingdom of God there is no place for class division, from which the rich, but not the poor, benefit (see below, p. 98). The eschatology of the Gospels is a well-trodden field, and disputes will no doubt continue. What can be said with certainty is that it is rooted in the political ethics of the Old Testament. The Testaments speak with one voice on the issue of social justice.

A far more spectacular development of this tradition is found in the climax of the book of Revelation. The "new Jerusalem" (Rev. 21:1–22:5) is a portrayal of the perfection of cosmic justice in the form of a city. It depends for many of its features on Isaiah 60, especially the presence of the glory of God as light (Rev. 21:23; 22:5; cf. Isa. 60:1–2, 19–20), the coming of the nations and their bringing of their treasures into it (Rev. 21:24, 26; cf. Isa. 60:6–11, 13), and the ever-open gates (Rev. 21:25; cf. Isa. 60:11). But there is a vital difference. Isaiah 60 represents Jerusalem as an imperial capital receiving tribute and captives from the nations. It is another picture of the reversal of fates, since Jerusalem at the time of writing was forced to pay tribute to an imperial power. But the account in Revelation makes it clear right at the start that the new Jerusalem is not to be an imperial mistress sucking the defeated nations dry. If oppressor and oppressed simply change places, that is not justice, popular as it might be with the oppressed. Rather, Rev. 21:3 quotes words frequently found in one form or another in the OT concerning Israel as YHWH's people (see Lev. 26:11–12; cf. 2 Chr. 6:18; Ezek. 37:27; Zech. 2:10), and applies them to the whole human race:

"He will dwell with them, and they shall be his *peoples*" – plural! Many textual authorities have "people", but this should be rejected on the standard principle that the harder reading is preferable. The nations will not be subordinate, they will all be part of the community of the new Jerusalem, and they will benefit from its goodness (22:2). Its enormous size (21:15–17) is appropriate to this function. The only people excluded are those whose activities are incompatible with the character of the city (21:27).

But the new Jerusalem can only come to earth when the earth is ready for it. Jerusalem can only be built when Babylon has been destroyed and all powers of evil have been defeated (Rev. 18–20). The drama of the fall of Babylon the great in Revelation 18 makes it very clear what kind of city Babylon is. It is an imperial power with client kings (18:3, 9; 17:2), and the primary object of its life is to live in luxury. The tribute that it gouges out of its subjects (not specifically mentioned, but no contemporary reader could be unaware of where its money came from) is used to pay for luxury goods (including the lives of human beings, 18:13), and thus to provide a living for merchants and sailors (18:11–19). The favours the "harlot" offers to the ruling classes of the empire are bought at a very high price (see Bauckham 1993: 338–83, who shows that the list of imports is an accurate one, though suggested by the list of Tyre's merchandise in Ezek. 27:12–24.) And this is the same power that persecutes the church (17:6; 19:2). This is the very picture of injustice on a world-wide scale, and the fall of Babylon arouses one of the great hymns of praise of Revelation (19:1–5).

It is clearly not wrong to say that Babylon stands for Rome. But it is not a mere token for the current imperial city. The object of using the name Babylon is to link Rome with the imperial power celebrated and execrated in Scripture. Thus Babylon becomes a universal symbol, which stands for the whole institution of oppressive imperial power, and in Babylon that whole system is comprehensively condemned and destroyed (Caird 1966: 222, 232).

The Permanent Significance of the Prophets

What the prophets teach us above all is that social and economic relationships are moral relationships, so that it is possible to speak of social *justice*. Historically, this has been the way in which they have influenced thinking about social justice in Jewish and Christian communities. Whenever readers of the prophets have found themselves in situations where the powerful have coerced and cheated the weak out of their wealth and their rights, they have responded out of their moral perception that this kind of action is wrong. Their resolve has been strengthened to stand up for the victims, and their sympathy deepened by the realization that these, these now today, are the poor whom YHWH's justice protects.

It is possible to argue that the prophets' approach is naïve in its lack of analysis and structural criticism, though it would be anachronistic to demand those skills of them themselves. Some modern thinkers have concluded that looking at social and economic relations as a system excludes moral considerations. There are plenty of commentators ready to tell us that these do not apply to the global economy, or at least that our morality has to be of the utilitarian variety, in which the "happiness (income?) of the greatest number" comes before the livelihood of an individual. (For a critical discussion of utilitarianism see Sandel 2009: 31–57.) We are told – still – that "there is no alternative", that to compete on a global scale requires "flexibility", that is fewer and less easily gained rights for the least well-paid workers, and the right of global capitalism to seek out the places where the lowest wages are paid (compatible with the skills required), so as to be able to sell at the lowest price and still make a profit; while the odium of taking jobs and undercutting wages can be diverted on to the heads of immigrants. But the prophets, for all their naivety, indeed because of their alleged naivety, "remind us that economic necessity is an abstraction that ignores the fact that people suffer because other people take decisions which affect them, and that decision-makers are morally responsible" (Houston 2008: 98), and may rightly be held to account for their decisions – to God if to no one else.

Questioning

If the Old Testament prophets were right in their assessment of justice in the human realm, the conception of God's justice in their words, at least as they have been edited and applied, must be adjudged deeply questionable. Consider these two points. In the first place, in their textual context, the words of the prophets are mostly addressed to whole peoples: "For three transgressions of *Israel*, and for four ... Hear this word that YHWH has spoken against you, *Israelites*, against the whole family that I brought up from Egypt" (Amos 2:6; 3:1); "Go and say to *this people ...*" (Isa. 6:9); and many other examples could be found.

Second, the principal weapon that the prophets place in God's hands to avenge the victims of oppression is war. And war is a disaster for both poor and rich. It is true that the prophets were thinking especially of deportation, the instrument of imperial policy deployed by both Assyrians and Babylonians to destroy the cadres of rebel vassals and deprive them of their power bases; and deportation was applied mostly to the urban classes, not only the upper classes, but also skilled craftsmen, according to 2 Kgs 24:14. But country people also suffered severely. Armies lived off the land that they invaded, and what they did not steal they burnt. Villagers must have died in their thousands of hunger and disease. Archaeological surveys show that there was a catastrophic fall in the population of Judah after the Babylonian invasions, though the area of Benjamin, north of Jerusalem, seems to have largely escaped (Middlemas 2005: 37–48; Faust 2003). Clearly the repeated visions of catastrophe in the book of Revelation, imaginary though they are, are at least equally problematic.

There are likely to be two aspects to doing "justice and right" in a situation of injustice. Putting an end to oppression may involve punishing the oppressor, in other words it includes retributive justice, but it must unquestionably also involve delivering the victims of oppression and giving them new life. But the narrative of justice presented by the prophets, in so far as it depends on war to achieve some rough approximation to justice, fails to achieve this, the main point of the exercise. There have been efforts to evade this unwelcome conclusion, but in my view they are not convincing. The last words of Amos (9:13–15), and comparable passages in other prophets, have been read by some as offering a prosperous future to the rural people of Israel after being freed of their urban oppressors (so Coote 1981: 121–27); but also after invading armies have consumed their crops and burnt their fields and houses! Others have argued that the entire people are complicit in the oppressive system; for example, Daniel Carroll argues from the passages attacking the worship of Israel in Amos that the temple cult gave sanction to the oppressive system, which in its turn kept the cult going, and hence everyone who joined in the cult was complicit (Carroll 1992: 209–10, 219, 273–77; similarly Marlow 2009: 150–52). It is unlikely, however, that poor people could have done so in any great numbers, since it meant making a pilgrimage and leaving one's work.

The problem is rather deeper than it seems at first sight. For, after all, the wars, invasions and deportations are a historical fact, and it is a historical fact that people suffered in them indiscriminately. This is no mere mistake by an over-enthusiastic prophet or over-systematizing editor. These things really happened.

The theological *mistake* was to make this indiscriminate suffering by real people a punishment for the sins of some of them. This could only be defended by invoking a doctrine of corporate responsibility, in which the evil done in a community is shared by all its members, as apparently expressed, for example, in the Decalogue, Exod. 20:5, or in Exod. 34:7 or in the story of Achan in Joshua 7. Yet at the very time the prophets were active, and even before their books reached their final shape, this idea was being strongly questioned. In Deuteronomy it is forbidden to punish a whole family for one person's crime (Deut. 24:16). Obviously this is because it is manifestly *unjust* – against "natural" justice – and also, of course, because it was sometimes actually being done. Abraham's wrestling with YHWH in Genesis 18 over the fate of Sodom concerns precisely this question: "Should not the Judge of all the earth *do justice?*", by not destroying just persons with the unjust. Ezekiel (14:12–20; 18) raises similar questions. (For a recent discussion of the idea of corporate responsibility in the Old Testament, see Kaminsky 1995.)

The theological *problem* is precisely that this suffering *was* indiscriminate, and the ancient and comforting doctrine of act and consequence was totally at a loss before it. Even less comprehensive suffering elicited bitter protests from the psalmists, who frequently charge YHWH with ignoring their plight, or even the prosperity of oppressors (Psalm 73). Generally, however, the justice of God is reasserted before the end of the psalm is reached: so Ps. 73:17–20; or e.g. 22:21b–24.

The book of Job wrestles with this problem, and is less easily satisfied. Its wrestling, as we have seen, is sharply relevant to the issue of *social* justice. Job is able to present counter-narratives to his friends' confident assertions of the sorry fate of oppressors: the wicked oppressor who lives a pleasant life and goes to an honoured grave accompanied by great troops of mourners (Job 21), or the wretched starving landless rural workers whose fate God ignores (Job 24:1–12). We saw earlier that the friends' doctrine is (potentially) ideological in that it justifies a social order in which the exploitation of the poor is possible, and perhaps frequent. It may reconcile the victims to their fate, in that they are assured that the oppression cannot last long, and the order of justice will quickly be restored. Thus once the act-consequence link is questioned, as it is by Job (and Ecclesiastes), the social order must become equally questionable. If God does *not* watch over the fairness of the social order, the poor are left to rely on paternalism and patronage *without* divine regulation, and this is decidedly unreliable. Perhaps this may push them to a different conception of just order, one in which the poor are not dependent on patrons and kings, in which hierarchy is eliminated and people do not need protection because they are a co-operative community of equals. For this we must wait until Chapter 5.

Chapter 4

THE STORY OF THE EXODUS: JUSTICE AS FAITHFULNESS

In the liberation theology of Latin America, the paradigm of God's liberation is the exodus, God's deliverance of the people of Israel from Egypt (e.g. Gutiérrez 1988; Croatto 1981). It is generally taken for granted that liberation is justice, given that slavery is the supreme example of injustice. José Miranda, who in fact takes justice rather than liberation as his leitmotif, analyses parts of the exodus story in several places in his *Marx and the Bible* as examples of God's response to injustice (Miranda 1977: esp. 78–89).

Probably the main reason for the central place taken by this story is the fact that the Old Testament itself presents it as a key founding narrative of Israel; not, however, in the sense that the people is actually created by these events, for it already exists (Exod. 1:7), and is recognized as such by the Pharaoh (Exod. 1:9: "the people of the children of Israel"). As all readers realize, even if they start with Exodus, this story has a pre-history. Israel is YHWH's people (Exod. 3:7) because he knows Abraham, Isaac and Jacob, Israel's ancestors (Exod. 3:6), and according to Genesis and to Exod. 2:24 he has made a covenant with them, a covenant which binds him to remember their descendants. The story is a founding narrative because it relates the events which establish the relationship of Israel and YHWH in the form which they are to take ever after (Exod. 3:15). YHWH "brings out" his people Israel, by the agency of Moses, "with a mighty hand and an outstretched arm", from their state of servitude to the king and people of Egypt, destroying their enemies in the Red Sea, and brings them to the mountain of God in the wilderness, where he makes a covenant with them, according to which they will be his holy people, his unique treasure (*segulla*, Exod. 19:5, cf. Deut. 7:6), on condition that they obey his commandments. The commandments themselves give as their leading requirement that Israel should have no other god. This covenant is accepted by Israel, but the "bringing in" of Israel to the land designated for them by YHWH is delayed by their disobedience; they wander in the wilderness for 40 years, before entering the land under the leadership of Joshua and destroying or driving out the inhabitants.

These basic elements of the story determine most theologically significant references to them in the rest of the Bible. The story as told in Exodus, however, is much more elaborate, especially because of the "plagues" narrative, which delays the dénouement by several chapters. This is referred to in some late "historical" psalms (Ps. 78:42–51; 105:26–36), but it is not clear whether the repeated references to YHWH's "mighty hand" in Deuteronomy (e.g. 6:21; 7:8) presuppose this narrative. It may well refer only to the miracle at the sea. The distinctive feature of the story in Exodus is the repeated attempt by Pharaoh to prevent the Israelites' exodus, frustrated by increasingly violent and dramatic blows of power from YHWH, but, extraordinarily, motivated also on each occasion by YHWH, who "hardens Pharaoh's heart".

Now, a number of investigations of this theologically difficult feature have in various ways come to the conclusion that it can only be accounted for on the understanding that YHWH is engaged in a struggle with Pharaoh to prove his own deity, to vindicate his rule over all the earth (cf. Exod. 9:16), that "they may know that I am YHWH" (Exod. 7:5, 17, etc.) (Gunn 1982; Durham 1987: 96; Gowan 1994: 131–40; Brueggemann 1995; Houston 2001a: 74; 2007: 20–25). It is only thus that there can be any moral justification for his compelling Pharaoh not only to act against his own interests but even to delay the ultimate liberation of the Israelites. However, the strategy YHWH pursues is calculated actually to prevent Pharaoh from "knowing that [he is] YHWH", since it blinds him to the truth of the situation. At Exod. 14:4 the final "that they may know…" must be intended ironically: if they ever know it, they know it as they meet their deaths. Thus in reality the strategy is not to enlighten Pharaoh but to triumph over him, to prove himself God of all the earth in the eyes of the Israelites (Exod. 14:31), if no one else.

Have I then made a mistake in placing the exodus story under a different heading from that of cosmic justice in creation? The act of delivering the people of Israel from cruel and unmerited forced labour is, in the first place, in itself a proper act of justice in the sense dealt with in the last chapter. It returns the relationships between the two peoples to equity, and wipes out an outrage like those denounced by Micah (3:9–10) and Jeremiah (22:13–14), only on a far larger scale. It is an act of justice demanded of YHWH as world ruler, if he is to "judge the world with equity". In the second place, YHWH is only able to do this because he is the creator and the controller of the natural elements (cf. Exod. 4:11). In the third place, his action against Pharaoh, making him dance like a puppet to his tune, is solely motivated by his need to prove himself world ruler.

All this is true, and a full analysis of the exodus story must include this aspect of YHWH's motivation. Yet there are other clues in the story that lead in a different direction. In principle, the ruler of the world, like the ruler of a state, should be impartial between his subjects. Impartiality in judging is a virtue emphasized in the Torah. Judges are not to be diverted from the path of justice by the wealth or status of those who appear before them, the number of their supporters or their bribes: Exod. 23:3, 6–8; Lev. 19:15; Deut. 16:18–20. Nor, significantly, are they to be influenced by personal favour for one of the parties: this is the meaning of the language of "respect of persons" (*ns'/nkr panim*; NRSV "show partiality"): Lev. 19:15; Deut. 1:17; 16:19. And Deut. 10:17–18 asserts that YHWH himself is the model judge, who "does not show partiality, does not take bribes, and does justice to the orphan and widow". The orphan and widow (and alien) are the type examples of people who have no connections or status, and who are therefore likely to get a raw deal from a corrupt judge or simply one who is not careful to judge fairly (as in Lk 18:2–4).

It would therefore be expected that any enslaved people would receive the same treatment from the judge of all the earth as Israel does. Yet if one is to judge from the language used when YHWH first appears on the scene in the Exodus story, he is anything but careful to avoid "respect of persons". "I have seen the affliction of *my people* in Egypt ... bring *my people*, the Israelites, out of Egypt!" (Exod. 3:7, 10). Miranda passionately denies that this expresses YHWH's motivation, citing the many occasions from Abel onwards on which YHWH responds to the cry of the oppressed in the absence of any pre-existing relationship (Miranda 1977: 89; see Houston 2008: 207–08). But why then does he mention that relationship? And this type of expression is repeated (Exod. 3:13, 15, 16), most significantly in Exod. 4:22–23: "Israel is my first-born son ..." Brueggemann (1997: 245) compares Hos. 11:1–3.

And YHWH's actions, not merely his words, are portrayed as partial towards Israel and indifferent to the sufferings of other nations. The "plagues" narrative, I have suggested, is motivated by YHWH's need to prove himself as God of all the earth. This should imply impartiality between different groups of oppressed people. But a repeated motif of the plagues is the distinction made between the Israelites and the Egyptians; the Egyptians suffer, while the Israelites observe events from a safe distance. This cannot be, as Brueggemann suggests (1995: 44–47), because the Egyptians are the oppressors and the Israelites the victims, because

Egyptians suffer *whether or not* they are oppressors. The slave-girl who grinds corn loses her first-born, and so do the prisoner in the dungeon and the domestic animals (Exod. 11:5; 12:29). These are victims of the Egyptian machine of exploitation equally with the Israelites. They suffer for no other reason than that they are Egyptian. YHWH's choice of targets is guided not at all by the motive of redressing oppression, but solely by his partiality for Israel as a nation, rooted, according to the Pentateuchal narrative, in his initial commitment to the ancestors (Houston 2007: 23–24).

And this is to say nothing of the eventual dispossession and massacre of the existing inhabitants of the land that YHWH designates as Israel's in Exod. 3:8. The text does offer justifications for this, especially that of their idolatry, which might become a "snare" for the Israelites (Exod. 23:33; Deut. 7:4, 6, 25–26), and a threat to their identity and existence. As Knierim points out, "the reference to the sins of the Canaanites … is not a rationale for justice independent of the theology of Israel's exclusive election. It depends on and serves that theology" (Knierim 1995: 98).

It thus becomes clear that the actions of YHWH in the Exodus story are motivated primarily by his commitment to Israel in an exclusive partnership, and only in the second place by his need to prove himself as world ruler.

Clearly there are ideological motives at work in the composition of this story. As I stated at the outset, this is one of the key founding narratives of the nation, so it is understandable that YHWH is represented as being partial to Israel. The story in some form may have served originally to justify the domination of the kingdom of Israel and the privilege it gave to Israelites over non-Israelite ethnic groups in the land: it was they and they alone, it would seem, who were free of demeaning labour service to the state (Houston 2008: 39). At a later stage it assured the Jewish people, now very much a subjugated minority, of their privileged status in the eyes of God, justifying the exclusive attitude taken towards other groups in order to defend the people's identity (cf. Ezra 9).

But it also served, in a somewhat contrary way, to motivate exhortations of Israelite/Jewish freemen to fair treatment of fellow-Israelites and resident aliens who were dependent on them. "Remember that you were a slave in Egypt, and YHWH your God brought you out from there with a strong hand and an outstretched arm", urges the commandment requiring Sabbath rest for slaves (Deut. 5:15), and likewise that requiring the release of a Hebrew slave after six years' service (Deut. 15:15). And "you were aliens in Egypt", YHWH reminds the Israelites when he forbids them to oppress aliens (Exod. 22:21; 23:9). They are thus both urged to imitate YHWH's gracious mercy to themselves and reminded of their solidarity with all members of the community, including those who are without honour in conventional thinking – like those "aliens" who had been made to suffer forced labour in the time of the kingdom of Israel. As so often, the tradition is turned in different directions in different contexts. In this application, the focus is on YHWH's gracious act of justice rather than on the identity and privilege of Israel.

But is the exodus really an act of justice? – a question that must be taken seriously when favouritism is viewed as injustice, as in the Torah sentences quoted earlier. I have noted elsewhere that the Hebrew word *tsedaqa*, which I have been translating as "right", though the usual translation is the archaic "righteousness", is frequently used in the Psalms and in Isaiah 40–55 in connection with YHWH's gracious acts of salvation towards Israel or (in the Psalms) an individual worshipper (Houston 2008: 211–14). In modern translations it is often, and properly, translated in these contexts "deliverance", "victory", "salvation", or "vindication" (e.g. NRSV at Isa. 46:13; 51:5, 6, 8; Ps. 98:2). But I argue that it is nevertheless an ethical term, implying that the salvation that YHWH gives is a right action. The best evidence for this is in the Psalms where it appears alongside *hesed* (NRSV usually "steadfast love"), which may be defined as an attitude or an action stemming from it which is "a beneficent action performed, in the context of a deep and enduring commitment between two persons or parties, by one who is able to render assistance to the needy party who in the circumstances is unable to help him- or herself" (Clark 1993: 267). Thus Psalm 89 defines the commitment of YHWH to David as *hesed* (Ps. 89:1, 2, 24, 33, etc.). So when these two words appear together, it will generally be in the context of such a permanent commitment between two parties, and they will point together to faithful and saving action on the part of God in favour of the human party: for example in Ps. 103:17–18 "YHWH's *tsedaqa* is his faithful saving grace, as his *hesed* is his committed and compassionate action to help" "those who keep his covenant and remember to do his commandments" (Houston 2008: 213). Again in Ps. 143:11–12 YHWH's *tsedaqa* is his "salvation" or "saving grace" within the context of his committed relationship with the one who speaks. Most remarkable (and significant for what we shall be saying about justification in Paul later on) is Ps. 51:14, where the penitent pleading for forgiveness defines it as "your salvation" and "your righteousness" (*tsedaqa*, NRSV "deliverance"). It will be *right* for YHWH to grant the plea because of his personal commitment to the penitent, indicated in the opening invocation "Have mercy upon me according to your *hesed*" (v. 1).

It seems clear, therefore, that the OT recognizes a strong moral obligation arising from personal commitment between two persons or parties. It is unsurprising that acts arising from such a commitment should be called "right", and at least reasonable that in English they should be called "just", although the word *mishpat* (judgement, justice) is not generally used alongside *tsedaqa* in this connection as it is in relation to social justice and forensic justice. For a just person is defined in the classical tradition which we have also inherited as, among other things, one who keeps promises, pays debts and maintains personal obligations. Sen (2009: 160) draws attention to some modern discussions of the distinctive ethical importance of relationships, such as the responsibility of parents to their children. That YHWH should deliver Israel from servitude in Egypt is entirely in line with this understanding of justice, and it makes understandable any incidental *unavoidable* harm to other parties. The difficulty in the story of the exodus as it is told is that much of this harm is not unavoidable in YHWH's fulfilment of his obligations to Israel as such, but arises from a confusion of YHWH's two roles as world ruler and protector of Israel – an unethical confusion, one is bound to observe (Houston 2007: 25).

This does not in any way undermine the validity of this concept of justice in its own right. It arises from well-defined social situations, on which the story of YHWH's dealings with Israel is modelled, and which make it believable to its original hearers. In Isa. 40–55 YHWH sometimes calls himself "your redeemer"; "redeemer" is *go'el*, denoting the relative in the *mishpaha* on whom lay the obligation of buying back alienated family property, or family members who had slipped into slavery (Lev. 25:25, 47–52; Ruth 3:9, 12–13; 4:1–6; Jer. 32:6–8). It is clear from Ruth 4:6 that this obligation was not absolute, and could be discharged by different people as they were able. This is in line with Hans Kippenberg's observation that in most pre-modern societies obligations are not dictated by law and contract, but arise out of a network of reciprocal relationships creating obligations of solidarity, which can be discharged as and when required (Kippenberg 1982: 32).

There is a similarity between the role of *go'el* and that of patron, the main differences being that the patron is always relatively wealthy and influential, is not a member of the family, and is chosen by the client initially, rather than being indicated by custom. Normally the patronal relationship is one of the type defined by Kippenberg: a reciprocal relationship creating an obligation of solidarity which is not defined by law or contract (Eisenstadt and Roniger 1984). When Ruth decides to glean in Boaz' field, and Boaz bestows his gracious recognition on her (Ruth 2:8–13), a relationship of patronage is set up – at this point the question of Boaz becoming *go'el* to Naomi has not been raised. The relationship of patronage is an exclusive one on the side of the client, that is, while the patron may have more than one client, perhaps very many, depending on his[1] wealth – Job portrays himself as patron to the entire town (Job 29:7–17) – the client has one patron, and cannot play off several patrons against each other. This is illustrated by Boaz' warning to Ruth not to glean in any other field (Ruth 2:8).

Although no law or contract defines the duties of patron and client to each other, once the relationship exists there are obligations that both sides must take seriously. The client must support and serve the patron, and the patron must provide assistance and support when it is asked for. But the patron has greater freedom than the client in deciding how to fulfil them. The client must come at the patron's call; the patron can decide how exactly to support the client, and by how much. He can also decide, if so minded, to call in his debts and reduce his client to debt-bondage if he cannot pay. The role of patron is one which can be played with generosity or with meanness, with genuine concern for the client's needs, or mainly with concern for the patron's own interests, whether his honour or his bank balance. We shall see later that one of the major concerns of the moral teaching of the Old Testament is to inculcate the generous interpretation of a patron's responsibility.

The key term which defines the virtue of a client who is faithful to his or her patron, and especially of a patron who cares for his client and gives whatever support the client may need, promptly and ungrudgingly, is *hesed*. It is largely because of the unfamiliarity of relationships of this type in the modern West that we find this word difficult to translate, being uncertain whether it relates to an obligation, resulting in such translations as "[covenant] loyalty", or denotes spontaneous generosity. The ancient versions, and the older English ones, went in the latter direction; the Septuagint has *eleos*, "mercy", while the KJV has "loving kindness" and the NRSV often "steadfast love", which is perhaps a compromise. The fact is that it is both, for the patron is obliged and yet can decide how and when to fulfil the obligation.

---

1. Patrons are normally male, probably always in ancient Israel and Judah.

Covenant

Although in everyday affairs patrons and clients were not normally bound by any formal promises or contracts, there are exceptions. Patronage was an institution also in international affairs: vassal kings were clients of their suzerains (the Romans actually called them *clientes*). Unlike private clients, who sought out patrons, vassals were generally made clients after a war of conquest. In the ancient Near East their obligations were defined and their loyalty secured by treaty. The word for "treaty" in Hebrew is *berit*, which in private and religious contexts is generally translated "covenant". A covenant is a solemn undertaking defining the relationship between two parties, in which one or both take oaths to perform certain duties. It has been argued that forms of covenant in the Bible are based on the standard formulae of contemporary vassal treaties; but others have disputed this (first in Mendenhall 1954; see McCarthy 1972; Nicholson 1986).

In Genesis YHWH binds himself by covenant to be Abraham's God, and to give him descendants and the land of Canaan (Genesis 15; 17). To a large extent, as David Clines argues (Clines 1978, 1997), the story of the Pentateuch can be understood as that of the steps YHWH takes to fulfil these promises. The covenant made at Sinai in Exodus 24 lays the balance of obligation on Israel. In effect, it formalizes the exclusive relationship of the client Israel with the patron YHWH, who has already acted for them with *hesed* and *tsedaqa* by delivering them from Egypt. The leading requirement is that they should acknowledge YHWH as their only God (Exod. 20:2–6). Of course, there are other requirements as well (Exod. 20–23), but there is no doubt about the leading place of the command of exclusivity. Each party is thereby permanently committed to the other, and it is "just" or "right" for Israel to remain loyal to YHWH and obey his commands, and for YHWH to give his blessing to Israel. See, for example, Deut. 6:25: "We shall be in the right ['it will be *tsedaqa* for us'], if we take care to observe this entire commandment before YHWH our God, as he has commanded us."

A God Compassionate and Gracious

We can develop our understanding of different aspects of God's justice and grace towards Israel through a study of the remarkable narrative in Exodus 32–34, which at the same time presents Moses as the model of the faithful patron of his people. The text is likely to be the result of a complex history, but it is perfectly possible to make sense of it as it stands (see the perceptive study by Walter Moberly (1983)). In this story, the people of Israel blatantly disobey the first requirement of the covenant they have just made by making and worshipping a "golden calf" in place of YHWH. The text in Exod. 32:1–6 is ambiguous about whether they have consciously abandoned YHWH for a false god, or whether they intend to worship YHWH under the form of the calf image, but as far as the narrator and YHWH himself (Exod. 32:8) are concerned it makes no difference. The Decalogue unambiguously forbids making an image to worship: it is equivalent to worshipping another god. The commandment against images (Exod. 20:4) is as it were folded into the commandment against having other gods, which continues in v. 5 (Zimmerli 1968: see Childs 1974: 406).

YHWH's response, speaking to Moses, is swift and devastating. "Let me alone, that my wrath may burn against them and consume them, and I shall make of you a great nation" (Exod. 32:10). There is a view that in saying this YHWH is hinting that he has no intention of actually destroying the people, and is ready to grant Moses' plea for them (e.g. Calvin 1854: iii. 341). But this view seems to be based on the theological dogma that God cannot change, and is contradicted by the specific statement in the text (32:14) that after Moses pleads for them, "YHWH changed his mind about the evil that he had said he would do to his people." We may leave the systematic theologians to argue about whether God does change God's mind. We can only make sense of the text by accepting that the character YHWH in the Bible does do so. Israel are actually in mortal danger; but on the other hand YHWH's "Let me alone" does hint that he is leaving the door ajar for Moses to try to change his mind. It is only because Moses has the courage to take up that offer that Israel are saved.

Let us be clear about one thing. YHWH is legally justified in threatening destruction to Israel for breaking the covenant. According to one of the many possible definitions of "justice", this is just. They have broken the leading stipulation of the covenant. In an analogous situation, an Assyrian king would certainly consider it right, if a vassal had rebelled, to remove him from his throne, devastate his country and deport his cadres. And the story makes the whole people responsible for this crime in a way which they would hardly have been in the case of a political infraction.

Moses, on the other hand, firmly ignores YHWH's tempting offer, and argues to his face against his proposal, and since he gets no answer from YHWH at this time (for the statement in v. 14 is made by the narrator to the reader, not by YHWH to Moses), he carries on arguing and negotiating over a period of days or weeks, until YHWH finally makes it clear (in 34:1) that he consents. Why does Moses do this? The narrator, sparing of psychological explanation as biblical narrators ever are, does not let us into the secret of his motivation. But it is reasonable to suppose that he feels identified with Israel and committed to them. No formal pact requires him to act in this way. It is his *hesed* that drives him to it, and his action is his justice towards his people. He is a model for the commanding officer who puts his own life in danger to protect his men, for the captain who goes down with his ship, for the head teacher who defends her children from attack in the media (Coats 1977).

He uses three arguments in 32:11–13 which are illuminating of the kinds of motivation expected of human patrons. First, he reminds YHWH of the effort he has expended in rescuing Israel from Egypt, "with great power and a strong hand". All that will go to waste if he destroys the people now. Second, he appeals to YHWH's honour: he will become a laughing stock with the Egyptians if he appears to have taken the people out of Egypt only to kill them. Third, and most seriously, he reminds him of the promises he has made to Abraham, Isaac and Jacob. This is a matter of justice, to honour his oath to his clients, even if Israel have not honoured theirs to him. But his speech contains not only arguments but also pathos, and the strongest element in it may be the words "Turn back from your anger, and revoke your intention of evil towards *your people*" (32:12). By calling the people "yours", Moses highlights the indissoluble connection between YHWH and Israel, his commitment to them which goes behind and beyond any explicit oaths and promises. To revoke that now would indeed be unjust, whatever they have done. A married couple do not normally remind each other of their marriage vows unless one of them has broken them or is in danger of doing so; what keeps them together is the unspoken love and commitment that grows between them through years of sharing life together.

But though YHWH is convinced by Moses' plea, he cannot say so yet. He is in a bind. It would indeed be humiliating to have to destroy Israel after all he has done for them. But it would be equally humiliating to submit to such a blatant insult as this. Either way, his honour will take a knock (Houston 2007: 15–17). His eventual solution to this dilemma, which comes in ch. 34, is one of the high points of the Old Testament.

It is clear from the beginning of the chapter that YHWH has decided to renew the relationship, since he gives Moses instructions to prepare to make new inscribed tablets to replace the ones that he had broken in 32:19. But it is the words he declares when he comes down on the mountain and joins Moses there that make it clear how he has reached this decision.

YHWH, YHWH, a God compassionate and gracious, slow to anger and rich in loving loyalty and faithfulness, who maintains his loving loyalty (*hesed*) with thousands and bears with wickedness, rebellion and offence; yet for all that does not wipe out guilt, for the wickedness of fathers punishing sons and grandsons, the third and the fourth generation (Exod. 34:6–7; translation as in Houston 2007: 15).

The solution is that "he is a compassionate God, and it is his glory, rather than a humiliation, to forgive; yet for all that he reserves the right to punish if he chooses" (Houston 2007: 16). In other words, forgiveness is an expression of his just conduct, his *hesed*, towards his people rather than a contradiction of it. Most of the terms used in this utterance, which was felt to be so important that it is quoted at least six times in other parts of the Old Testament, are ones which refer to a particular relationship rather than to one's dealings with people in general. The weight of the self-description falls on YHWH's *hesed* and his faithfulness or reliability ('*emet*, a term which frequently seconds *hesed*). His solidarity with Israel, his commitment to them, persists despite their gross offence, which would have given grounds for breaking it off. He will show mercy and help to them whenever it is required, and he can be relied on. Everything else in the description is related to that basic assertion, including *both* his reserving the right to punish *within* the relationship, as part of it, not by breaking it off, *and* his choosing to forgive whenever it is appropriate. There is no opposition between justice and mercy: mercy and punishment are both ways in which YHWH's faithful saving power (*tsedaqa*) may be expressed, depending on the circumstances. The terms which head the self-description, *rahum* and *hannun*, emphasize YHWH's compassion and his gracious favour: his compassion for his people in trouble, a quality that he had already displayed when he saw them ill-used in Egypt, but which is now excited by the danger they are in from their own offence against him; and the favourable notice which he has given especially to Moses' unwearied efforts on their behalf. They are a clear signal that YHWH has decided that enough punishment has been exacted, and now is the time to forgive, and therefore that his loyalty to his people now demands that he should reinstate the covenant. (See Houston 2007: 16–17).

Nevertheless forgiveness remains a choice rather than a requirement. Indeed in the Old Testament (Hebrew canon), in contrast to the New, it is never presented as a moral requirement for human beings either, though there are a number of examples of forgiveness among Old Testament characters. David Reimer points to Esau's forgiveness of Jacob and David's relenting in his pursuit of Nabal at Abigail's plea, as well as the stories of

David and Saul and David and Absalom (Reimer 1996). The most striking example is that of Joseph, who after trying his brothers long enough is eventually constrained by his emotions to reveal himself to them (Genesis 42–45). In all these cases, there is no moral obligation to forgive (except perhaps in the case of David and Saul, where David regards Saul as inviolable because of his anointing as king, or at least professes to do so): it is a freely chosen act of grace.

The "Righteousness of God"

The same is true in the New Testament, which has much to say of God's forgiveness, and in the New Testament this is explicitly described as God's righteousness or justice (*dikaiosune*). A striking example before we come to the classic expression of this insight in Paul is the parable of "the labourers in the vineyard", Mt. 20:1–16. For this is explicitly a discussion of justice. The complaint of the workers who have worked all day is that the master is being *unfair*. "You have made them equal to us who have toiled all day in the blazing sun" (v. 12). The master's reply is that he is not being unfair, *ouk adiko se*, "I am not doing wrong to you", because a denarius was the wage agreed between them (though it must be said that in all such negotiations the boss has the whip hand; it is not an agreement between people of equal power). He has *chosen* to give the same to the latecomers: it is an act of gracious generosity, because otherwise they will be unable to put bread in their families' mouths. He asks "Are you envious because I am good (or 'kind', *agathos*)" – not "just (*dikaios*)" (v. 15). But such acts of gracious generosity are of the essence of God's *tsedaqa*. Justice cannot be restricted to the observance of formal agreements, or on the other hand to the calculation of proportional rewards for work done. To feed the hungry because they are hungry is also justice, and to save the perishing is the just work of God.

It is in this context of God's *tsedaqa* as his faithful saving power that we should interpret Paul's discussions of God's *dikaiosune*, generally "righteousness", a word that usually translates *tsedaqa* in the LXX. The epistle to the Romans is best understood if we realize that God's mercy and forgiveness are not opposed to God's *dikaiosune* or "righteousness", but an expression of it. Thus in the key passage Rom. 3:21–26, after Paul has come to the conclusion that "no living thing can be justified before him" (a quotation from Ps. 143:2), "the righteousness of God" is made known "through faith in Jesus Christ" (or "through the faithfulness of Jesus Christ": see Dunn 1988: 166–67 and Downing 2010). It is difficult to disentangle the complex series of clauses and phrases that follows, but it is clear enough that for Paul the achievement of God's righteousness is to "justify", to "make or declare just or righteous" those who have been unable to justify themselves, but have put their trust in Jesus Christ. It seems reasonable to suggest that Paul is speaking of God's "faithful saving power", through which he "justifies" or forgives the ungodly, exactly as in Ps. 51:14. James Dunn defines it, on v. 22, as "God's action on behalf of those to whom he has committed himself", which is almost exactly how I have defined the concept of justice operative in the exodus (Dunn 1988: 166).

The group to whom God is thus committed is no longer the same: Paul is concerned to emphasize that it is "all who believe, for there is no distinction" – that is, between Jew and Gentile. Yet the Old Testament background of the thought is emphasized, not only formally with the reference to "the law and the prophets" that witness to God's righteousness (v. 21), but also in content, when Paul refers to "the redemption in Christ Jesus" (v. 24), using the noun *apolutrosis*, which recalls the frequent use of *lutroun* in the LXX with reference to God's redemption of Israel, in the exodus (e.g. Deut. 7:8), and from exile (e.g. Isa. 41:14) (Dunn 1988: 169). Verses 25–26 clarify the manner of the redemption: it is through Christ's sacrificial death, which demonstrates, according to Dunn, that God's action is "in fulfilment of the obligation he took upon himself as covenant God of Israel", affording a means of expiation where sins had been left unpunished. God's justice therefore follows the same broad model as in Exodus 32–34. Sins have not been ignored, but at the key moment, in this case at the death of Christ, sinners have been justified. In this way God has shown that God is just, not acting arbitrarily any more than the master in the parable, but delivering those who have faith in Christ by righteous and faithful saving power.

These reflections are obviously of key importance for Christian theology; but they ought also to be regarded as significant for any radical thinking about criminal justice. Suppose that in reality and not merely in theory the object of justice were to reconcile the criminal with the community? But an essential presupposition of this would be that the state, representing the community, should regard itself as committed to the criminal, however obnoxious, simply as a member of the community, and that its aim should be by whatever means to *justify* the criminal, not in the sense of remitting punishment, but designing the punishment to bring him or her into reconciliation with the victims and society in general. Taking up such an object would surely not have the result of the ratcheting up of prison sentences which is happening at the moment in the UK, or the slow annihilation of prisoners on death row, as in the USA. It surely would have the effect of making sentences more imaginative and money being spent on the probation service rather than on prisons. But this would still be justice! (See also below in ch. 7, p. 104.)

Teaching Justice to the Individual

One of the main objects of the legal and moral teaching of the Old Testament is to teach patrons to fulfil their obligations with generosity. Exod. 21:2–11 and 22:21–27 address a man (so gendered!) with power and resources, who can use them to the benefit of his poor neighbours or to exploit them (for details see Houston 2008: 105–18, as well as the commentaries). Much of this teaching is developed and expanded in Deuteronomy: see Deut. 15:7–18; 23:19–20; 24:6, 10–15, 17–22; and compare Lev. 19:9–10, 33–4; 25:35–43. In several places the writers of these texts must envisage a relationship of patronage type, rather than a general responsibility for the poor. One sign of this is the use of the phrase "with you" in Exod. 22:25[2] and Lev. 25:35, 39,[3] which implies that the poor person is in some way dependent on the addressee. Obviously the bonded labourer in Exod. 21:2–11 and Deut. 15:12–18 is in a dependent relationship, and this could well be a development from being a client, or a client's child. Another is the way in which Deut. 15:7–11 speaks of a single poor person whom you are to help. It is not speaking of general charity, but urges lending to a particular person for whom you have some responsibility.

But of course the responsibility of those whom God has blessed with prosperity is not limited to their relatives and clients. A sketch of the righteous person's life in the Psalms says, among other things: "They have distributed freely, they have given to the poor" (Ps. 112:1, 4, 5, 9 NRSV). Job declares he has not "withheld anything that the poor [plural] desired, or disappointed a widow; eaten my piece alone, without sharing it with a fatherless child; seen anyone perishing for lack of clothing or a poor person without covering, and his body has not been grateful to me, warmed by the fleece of my lambs" (Job 31:16–22). Biblical justice includes not only the discharge of specific obligations, but an unmeasured generosity. This is what is meant by the virtue of *hesed* when this generosity is extended to those one has a specific relationship with, whether of kinship or patronage. But it is clear that there is a broader duty of generosity to those who are in

2. The NRSV "among you" cannot be right, because "you" is singular here.
3. Here the NRSV correctly discerns the sense "dependent on you".

need, and a corresponding responsibility not to take advantage of the vulnerable: in the Old Testament the traditional examples are the alien, the widow and the fatherless. In the New Testament, the Sermon on the Mount goes even further: while Matt. 5:42 agrees with Deut. 15:7–11 on lending to those in need, the preceding verses say: "Do not resist a wicked person; but if someone strikes you on the right cheek, turn the other [giving up the man of honour's right of revenge]; if someone sues you for your tunic, let him have your cloak as well; and if anyone conscripts you for one mile, go two miles with him" (Matt. 5:39–41).

Most biblical texts on generosity are moral exhortation rather than law in any formal sense; there are no sanctions, and in form they are personal address. Like the Bible in general, they take the existence of masters and slaves, poor and rich, free and dependent people for granted. Indeed Deut. 15:11 states expressly that "the poor will never cease to exist in the land". Leviticus 25, however, projects a utopian vision of a society without classes in which poverty is a temporary misfortune. The object of this teaching is not to show the way to an equal society (it is unlikely that this is the meaning of Deut. 15:4), but to educate the comfortably off in their responsibility to the less fortunate members of their communities. To that extent it has an ideological aspect: on the whole it confirms the comfortable in their position in society while reminding them of the serious moral dangers of meanness and hardheartedness; it accepts a class society while attempting to make the relationships between classes gentler and less exploitative. We shall see, however, that there are points in the teaching that, if taken seriously, tend to undermine the ideology.

We have seen the importance of debt in the hardening of social stratification and the fall of poor people into dependence. The subject is repeatedly addressed in these texts, and their teaching is well summed up in the warning in Exod. 22:25, "If you lend money to a poor person dependent on you, you shall not act like a moneylender." The Hebrew text is difficult (see Houston 2008: 110), but clearly the meaning is that you are not to behave oppressively, though the Hebrew *noshe* (NRSV "creditor") is of uncertain meaning. There are several references to the taking of objects as security, and the concern everywhere is that, while it is permissible to take security, the creditor should behave in a way which respects the dignity and well-being of the debtor: a cloak should be returned at night (Exod. 22:26–7; Deut. 24:12–13), and a millstone should not be taken (Deut. 24:6), because flour ground at home was the staple diet; the creditor should not enter the debtor's house to seize the pledge (Deut. 24:10–11); widows should not be asked for security at all (Deut. 24:17). Interest should not be charged on loans for the relief of poverty (Exod. 22:25; Lev. 25:36–37; Deut. 23:19–20). The significance of this can be gauged from what we know of interest rates in the ancient Near East; for example the laws of Hammurabi prescribe limits of 20% on a loan of silver and 33% on grain. These rates are for the duration of the loan; but this would normally be a year or less.

If the creditor observed these restrictions, borrowing would be a slightly less painful experience. But they do not in themselves guarantee that the ultimate outcome will be any different. The teachers therefore also deal with the reality of bonded service for debt, and prescribe a six-year limit on it (Exod. 21:2 (restricted to men); Deut. 15:12); Deuteronomy adds an encouragement not to let the bonded labourer go without a generous "golden handshake" (Deut. 15:13–14). But at the same time they allow the bonded person to choose permanent slavery (Exod. 21:5–6; Deut. 15:16–17a), a not unlikely choice when the alternative is the uncertainties of casual wage-labour. As we have seen, the bonded labourer would usually be a child of the debtor. Leviticus deals rather with the case where the debtor himself (or herself?) is forced to the step of selling himself into bondage (Lev. 25:39–43; Lefebvre 2003: 307–14). This is why there is no seventh-year release here; instead the debtor is not to be treated as a slave, but "as a resident waged labourer" (Lefebvre 2003: 26). For the actual hired labourer the single instruction is to ensure that he is paid his wages on time (Deut. 24:14–15). As with many of the instructions to do with lending, the patron is urged to consider the sheer survival of the client: a mark, like the cloak that is to be returned because it doubles as the debtor's blanket, of the absolute poverty of many of those compelled to depend on the charity of their neighbours. There is nothing in these instructions that is likely to make a permanent difference to that.

The other pernicious outcome of debt was the loss of land. This was obviously felt to be a more intractable problem. The gleaning texts and the laws of the sabbatical year (Exod. 23.10–11; Lev. 25.1–7) offer a minimal sort of relief for the landless. It is of course quite inadequate (Bennett 2002), but doubtless better than nothing. The only text which directly addresses landlessness and provides a theoretical mechanism for dealing with it is the jubilee law of Lev. 25:8–22, which we shall look at in the next chapter.

Most of these instructions or exhortations are urged with persuasive rhetoric, and this is where their theological and ethical interest lies. The rhetoric attempts to overcome in various ways the resistance to appeals to generosity that may be expected from the comfortable. A number of different themes emerge in these "motive clauses", as they are known. Some we have already touched on. The promise of God's blessing if the instruction is obeyed (Deut. 15:10, 18; 23:20; 24:13, 19) or of God's vengeance if the wronged client appeals to heaven (Exod. 22:23–24, 27) draws on the theology of God as world ruler who maintains cosmic justice; but the note of the appeal of the victim interestingly dramatizes the theme, and links it with those many psalms which are precisely the appeal of the downtrodden. "Remember that you were a slave/alien in Egypt" we looked at above. But there are some new ones. There is an intense pathos in the exhortation in Deut. 15:7–11 to continue to lend to the needy even when the year of remission is near. Jeffries Hamilton (1992: 31–34) notes that it is created by the use of "somatic" language, metaphors from parts of the body: close fists and open hands, hard hearts and evil eyes (v. 9; "view with hostility" is the correct but dull NRSV translation).

But most significant for our purpose are the ways in which the needy person is characterized. Probably the oldest term, found in Exodus and in Deuteronomy, is "neighbour" (Exod. 22:26–27; Deut. 15:2; 24:10). This is a common term for the person with whom the person addressed by a law must deal. It is for example used in the commandments of the Decalogue against false witness and coveting. It implies common membership in a local community, and therefore equality in principle. In Deut. 15:2 there appears the stronger designation "brother" (NRSV "member of the community" or "another Israelite"), which is used repeatedly in that chapter and in subsequent chapters to refer to a fellow-member of the national community. It is used in 23:19–20, but not in ch. 24. It is then picked up and used several times in Leviticus 25. The power of this term on several counts should not be underestimated (Perlitt 1980; Houston 1995: 304–07; 2008: 182–84). (It is unfortunate that it is obscured by the NRSV in its drive for inclusive language.) It first of all packs an emotional punch far greater than "neighbour": one's brother, for a male in that culture, is the male to whom one is closest. It expresses "the common humanity of those who together live out of the liberating love of God" (Perlitt 1980: 42). Second, like "neighbour", only more strongly, it implies equality, membership of the community on the same terms. Third, as I have argued (Houston 1995: 306–07; 2008: 183–84), it defines the national community in the image of a family, or, to be more precise, as a clan or lineage, a *mishpaha*, a group related by kinship. The designation recalls the community of the tribal village, from which perhaps many of the hearers were not far removed, and so attempts to re-create a sense of solidarity in the fragmented society of the cities, with the intention of transforming patron-client relationships. Whomever I have such dealings with I should treat as a "brother" (or sister – see Deut. 15:12), that is, in the way pleaded for in Deut. 15:7–11 (and Lev.

25:35–43), with generosity and humanity rather than calculation and hardheartedness.

But I have already pointed out that these texts – Deut. 15:11 explicitly – assume that a class society will continue. There is thus in the thought of Deuteronomy 15 in particular a tension between the ethics of solidarity and the acknowledged social reality. What it calls its hearers to is humane conduct softening the harshness of a divided society; what the rhetoric conjures up is the ideal of a society of equals. This is what I mean by saying that there are points in the texts that undermine their ideology.

Leviticus 25 is ambiguous in a different way: it appears to presuppose that the institution of the jubilee will prevent the emergence of such a society, so that poverty will only be a temporary misfortune (Houston 2001b: 39–42; 2008: 197–99). And as Habel points out, it ignores the existence of landless peasants, hired labourers and exploiting creditors (Habel 1995: 112); but on the other hand the shifts to which impoverishment and bankruptcy will drive people are depicted accurately and in detail, which suggests that the reality of a class-divided society is in the mind of the writers even if not admitted in the text. Both texts point us forward, Leviticus less equivocally than Deuteronomy, to our third narrative of justice, the narrative of the society of equals.

But this does not mean that there is no permanent value in this teaching about treating one's subordinates with justice and humanity – justice as humanity. For we today are even further from that society of equals, whatever our pretensions, than ancient Israel was. Our democratic constitution gives an equal weight to every voice, in theory. But the truth is that we still have rulers (even if we mendaciously call them leaders!), there is still a structure of authority, in some ways more hierarchical because more bureaucratic. Even less are we equal in the workplace or in public administration, or in school. The worldwide triumph of capitalism subjects billions of people to the unaccountable direction of a few. Even if in some countries some workers have acquired substantial rights, in others the average worker is vulnerable to the whims, the abuse, the exploitation of a powerful employer. It would be strange to say that the teaching of these texts was out of date in these circumstances. On a global view, even the particular circumstances that they are concerned with are not at all out of date – lending for profit, debt bondage, exploitation of migrant workers, rural landlessness and destitution – they all still exist somewhere, some of them everywhere. Recently, we celebrated the bicentenary of the abolition of the slave trade in the British empire. But slavery still exists, in the UK also, and often in grimmer forms than the bonded domestic labour dealt with in the Old Testament texts.

Everyone who has control of someone else's destiny, everyone who has dependants who cannot or will not stand up for themselves, needs the teaching of these texts, needs to be taught: "Treat the other as a human being like yourself, a member of God's family, remember that you too owe your life to the grace of God, and if you abuse or exploit one who is in your power, beware of God's anger."

Chapter 5

The Story of Israel: Justice as a Community of Equals

Both the Prophets and the wisdom literature generally assume the existence and appropriateness of a hierarchical society. The object of prophetic denunciation in the social field is usually the abuse of their power by persons whose power is not criticized in principle (Houston 2008: 96, 136–38). But a strand of thought at variance with this can be traced primarily in the Torah. This may well have its roots in the traditional rural society of Israel and Judah, which was, as I have expressed it in the title of this chapter, a community of equals (above). This is not quite the same as an equal society. There is no detectable concern in the Torah or elsewhere for the material equality of all citizens. What there is is a conviction that all do or should stand on an equal footing, before God and before each other, and that this should be expressed in practical ways. Exactly who these "all" are is of course an important question. Later in the chapter we shall need to analyse the precise ways in which women, strangers and others, are included and excluded.

It is true, as we have seen, that in real life wealth or poverty made a substantial difference to the way in which anyone was treated by society. The Torah on the other hand expresses an ideal. Originally, as in Mesopotamia, the laws would not have been formulated in order to be applied by the courts. Rather, they were to be studied as models of justice (Jackson 1989: 187–88; 2006: 3–16). The ideals are those of the scribal and priestly class that wrote it, but these would to a large extent be shared with the people as a whole (Walzer 1987: 40–42). They may have been in the service of the ruling class, but they did not necessarily bend every nerve to support their material interests. Indeed, they may well have considered that their employers' interests were best served if they were encouraged to behave with justice and generosity to their subjects, and especially to have regard to popular views of fairness and justice, which extend to the conviction of fundamental equality. It is certainly true that the book of Proverbs, also a work of the scribal class, encourages the sense of *noblesse oblige* in its readers, who will mainly have been drawn from the ruling class (Kovacs 1974; Houston 2008: 123–24).

We have already come across one way in which this fundamental equality is expressed, in the use of "your brother" in Deut. 15:7–11 and other passages in Deuteronomy, and also in Leviticus 25. In this way the people of Israel are imagined as a family. It is true that the Hebrew extended family was not an equal society, being controlled by its patriarchal head, with its women and slaves and other unrelated household members clearly subordinate, and with obedience and respect being expected by parents from their children at any age. So of course the image is inexact, but it expresses no doubt how Hebrews, at least male ones, constructed their families in their minds, as a band of "brothers".

Another such expression can be detected in the Deuteronomic understanding of Israel as a people holy to YHWH. This is evidently understood to imply that every individual is holy: hence the instructions in Deut. 14:1–21 which prohibit individuals from mutilating themselves or eating unclean flesh, actions which would compromise their holiness (Nelson 2002: 174–82; Houston 1993: 241–44). In a similar way, but expressed somewhat differently, the Holiness strand in Leviticus demands such avoidances so that the people, and every individual in the people, should make and keep themselves holy (Lev. 19:2; 11:44–45; 19:26–31; 20:22–26). For the holiness writers the meaning of holiness extends also to the ethics of community living (Lev. 19:9–18, 32–36). Exod. 22:31 expresses the same idea. The holiness of members of Israel would not in itself imply that all were equal; but the idea is expressed in Exod. 19:6 in a striking and unique way which surely does so: "You are to me a kingdom of priests and a holy nation." "Kingdom of priests" *could* mean "a kingdom ruled by priests", but it is far more likely in this context to mean "a kingdom consisting of priests" (Propp 2006: 158). Nowhere else are all Israelites called priests, and the Torah is clear that only Levites are priests; the priestly writings restrict the office to the descendants of Aaron. Obviously the word is being used here in a metaphorical sense, in which all Israelites are holy through being close to YHWH, just as within Israel priests have a particular responsibility to maintain their holiness (Leviticus 21–22).

The Society of Equals in the Laws

Civil law in any society may suggest how the society's members are thought of as being related to each other. The body of laws and commandments in Exod. 20:22–23:33 (the so-called "Book of the Covenant"), probably the oldest of all the biblical law collections, includes a body of case law (21:2–22:17) that, according to Bernard Jackson, is best understood as offering models for the settling of disputes between individuals who are able to treat with each other on equal terms. Jackson speaks of "self-executing laws", that is, laws which do not need a judge to apply and enforce them (Jackson 1989: 197; 2006: 29–30). This would be true even of the provisions for release of debt slaves (21:5–6), and other laws on slavery (21:7–11, 20–21, 26–27), since the slave's own family would probably be living in the same place and able to monitor the treatment of their relative (Jackson 2006: 110–15). In any case, neither this body of law nor the others in the Torah should be understood as law in the modern sense, codes which define how courts are to deal with cases. It is clear from legal records that such a well-known "code" as that of Hammurabi was not used in this way. Rather, these ancient collections, outside the Bible and in it, are models which may instruct their readers about justice, but were not intended to constrain the way judges decided cases (Jackson 1989). This in no way reduces their value as evidence of how justice was understood.

Two clear distinctions have been noted between the biblical law collections and the Mesopotamian ones. One is that in contrast to the Mesopotamian "codes", there are no separate orders of society. For example Hammurabi's "code" presupposes that free adult male members of society are of two different kinds to which different rules apply. Less severe punishments are applied to an *awilu*, which literally means "man" but in this context means a member of the higher order of society, than to a *mushkenu*, literally a poor man. The biblical collections make no distinction of this kind. The priests might be described as an order, and they do have certain privileges in relation to sacred offerings, but as regards the civil law they are on an equal footing with lay people; they are not mentioned in the Covenant Code. As we have seen, the biblical laws recognize slavery, but so far as Israelites are concerned (the "Hebrew slave" in Exod. 21:2; Deut. 15:12; see Propp 2006: 186–88; Jackson 2006: 80–85), this is not intended as a permanent status but a time-limited position to work off a debt. It is also clear enough that in many situations women are treated differently from men, generally worse; we shall go into more detail about this below. The positive point which remains is that the family you are born into does not make any difference in the way the law affects you.

The other clear difference from Mesopotamian law that has been remarked is that property offences are treated less seriously than offences against the person. For example, in the Code of Hammurabi, capital punishment is frequently prescribed for theft (*CH* 7–11 (Richardson 2000:

44–47)). In the Book of the Covenant, the only place in the Torah where a penalty is prescribed for theft, a cattle rustler (doubtless standing for thieves in general) must pay double what he has taken if it is still in his possession, four times if he has slaughtered or sold it. If he cannot pay, he is to be sold as a slave – a severe punishment, but not to be compared with death. The householder is free of guilt if the thief breaks in at night and is killed, but not in the daytime (Exod. 22:1–4). On the other hand, kidnapping is a capital crime (Exod. 21:16). The kidnapper's usual object would be to make money by selling people as slaves, if he could not obtain a ransom. Deuteronomy goes a small step further in reprehending slavery by prohibiting the return of escaped slaves (Deut. 23:15–16; it is not clear whether this only applies to slaves from foreign parts). Murder is a capital crime (Exod. 21:12–14, etc.), and paying blood-money to the relatives as a way of escaping capital punishment is prohibited (Num. 35:31).

It is likely that this reflects the kind of weighting that popular sentiment would give to the two types of crime, a sentiment with close roots in the culture of the villages, which shows marked reserve about material display, while valuing persons equally (above, p. 22). The Mesopotamian "codes", on the other hand, emerge from a culture where urban living was of far greater antiquity, and, as we have seen, had developed hierarchical orders of society which valued some persons less than others, and therefore could easily be led to value their lives at less.

Deuteronomy

We saw in the last chapter how Deut. 15:7–11 and other passages giving moral guidance to those in a position to help or exploit their fellow-citizens are shot through with a tension between the explicit moral exhortation to be generous to the poor, since they will always exist, and the implication that they are fellow-citizens on an equal footing with you. But it is the implication of solidarity and equality that is more in accord with the overall socio-ethical standpoint of Deuteronomy: hence perhaps the (embarrassed or idealistic) added comment in Deut. 15:4–6 that if the commandments are obeyed, there will in fact be no poor in Israel, though the way this remark is developed makes it mean that the people as a whole will be well off, rather than that it will be equal.

The book of Deuteronomy is addressed to a relatively complex society, in the first instance, at least in an early form, to the cities of the kingdom of Judah, and it assumes the existence of social stratification, hired labour, debt bondage and various central institutions, not only the central sanctuary which it mandates, but a central government of some sort even in the absence of a king (17:8–13) and a national militia (20:1–9). Deuteronomy 16:18–18:22 gives instructions for the appointment or acceptance of national leadership cadres: judges, king, priests, prophet. Yet in spite of this it continues to hold in principle to the primitive equality of Israel, regardless of the fact that this may be little more than theoretical in existing conditions. Its general stance is that Israel is a people without hierarchies, who stand before God as free and equal individuals.

Thus, the covenant is made with all the people, including women, children and aliens, and indeed also including heads of tribes, elders and officials (Deut. 29:10–13; cf. 5:2–3). It is not made with these leaders and then mediated to the people. Further, the people are addressed to a large extent in the second person singular. What is the meaning of this? Is it that the people are thought of as a single person in solidarity? Or is it that at these points the text has in mind the actual individual who is required to obey the commandment? The answer must be that it is either or both, according to the context: at 7:17, "When you say to yourself, 'These nations are more numerous than I. How can I dispossess them?'..." it must be that Israel is thought of as a single person. But frequently it is plain that the law is concerned with the activities of individuals, and the individual is addressed, for example in 15:12: "When your Hebrew brother or sister is sold to you ..." This underlines that the responsibility for the keeping of the commandment, and thus for the security of the covenant, lies with each individual Israelite. A hierarchy of responsibility is not possible when the maintenance of the covenant is in the hands of every individual.

It is true that besides the appointment of judges and the recognition of the tribe of Levi as priests, with judicial powers (17:9, 12) as well as religious duties, many passages allow for the existence of elders in the towns and their authority in various judicial connections. But the elders are probably simply the heads of the local families, and the paragraph on the king is almost entirely devoted to restrictions on his activities: he is not to accumulate horses, wives or gold and silver, and must devote himself to the study of the Deuteronomic law. The object is "that his heart may not be exalted above his brethren, and that he may not turn aside from the commandment to left or right" (Deut. 17:20). This makes it clear that in principle the king is simply one of a body of equal "brethren", and he is not to behave in a way which would threaten that status. Chariot forces, marriage alliances and the accumulation of capital are all instruments of power in the hands of kings. The Deuteronomic ideal king is not to accumulate power over his fellow-citizens: is he a king at all? This is no doubt a utopian provision which lacked any serious possibility of being implemented; it is all the more important as giving an indication of the social ideals of the text.

A Community of Equal Landholders

Israel is conceived by the biblical text as a landholding people among whom the land is divided in equal shares – fair shares! This is implied in the account of the allocation of the land by Joshua, and in the jubilee law of Leviticus 25. Again, this fashions the people as a whole in the image of the egalitarian tribal village.

A preparatory text in Num. 33.50–56 for the account of the land distribution sets out the principles. Allocation is to be made by "families", i.e. *mishpahot*, and by lot. YHWH tells Moses to tell the Israelites, "you shall give a larger share to a larger *mishpaha*, and a smaller share to a smaller one" (v. 54). The account of the distribution made by Joshua in Josh. 13–19 follows these principles, and it is stated at the beginning of the description of each tribe's allocation that the distribution was made "by *mishpahot*", "family by family" (NRSV). Presumably the assumption is that the *mishpaha* will distribute the land in its possession to the extended families that make it up, again on the principle of larger shares to the larger families. It is emphasized that the tribe of Levi receives no land, but in compensation "their portion is YHWH", which in practical terms means that the tithes and offerings give them a living which makes up for the lack of land.

The socio-ethical assumptions of the jubilee law are illuminating. Leviticus 25 as a whole is concerned with the land, and the conditions on which it is held by Israel. The general principle of the law in Lev. 25.8–55 is that the land as a whole belongs to YHWH (v. 23), and is held at his will by individual Israelites, each of them probably understood as the head of an extended family, and no land can be permanently alienated; it must either be redeemed by the *go'el*, the nearest relative on the male side (v. 25), or the original landholder (v. 26), or revert to its original owner (or, presumably, to his heirs) at the jubilee, at the end of every 50 years, when "everyone" – every *man* (*'ish*) – "shall return to his landholding, and everyone to his *mishpaha*" (v. 10). The general effect is described as a "liberation", *deror*, a word also used of the liberation of slaves under Zedekiah in Jer. 34:8; according to Lev. 25:40–41, 54 the jubilee will include the liberation of Israelite slaves.

I have suggested that although this law has frequently been described as utopian, it is not impractical provided that its initial assumption is accepted, that Israel is a society without classes, without permanent rich and poor; poverty for a landholder of Israel is a temporary misfortune, to be rectified by the jubilee, at the latest. It is this assumption which is the truly utopian feature of the law (Houston 2001b: 39–42; 2008: 197–99). This text expresses in a clearer fashion than any other the understanding of the people of Israel as a community of equals. Every man possesses what the text describes as *'ahuzza*, a holding of land. If the initial distribution of land to the families of Israel was fair, in the sense that each received land in proportion to its size, then that fair distribution is restored at each jubilee, so that the essential equality of the land holdings is never permanently damaged.

Norman Habel argues that the society envisaged is not egalitarian in any sense of the word that we would recognize. Urban residents and landless rural workers, whether free hired labourers or slaves, are excluded from equal standing in a community based on land holding, as are all foreigners, whether resident or not (Habel 1995: 112). It is perfectly true that, although foreigners may become rich and possess slaves (Lev. 25:47), they cannot possess *'ahuzza*, and so are not full members of the community. It is also true that women and children are not visible parts of the community so far as this text is concerned. Doubtless, as Christopher Wright argues (Wright 1990: 124–25), the "man" of this text is understood as the head of a family, whose members share the produce of his holding, and are probably understood as sharing also his poverty, his reduction to dependency if that happens, and his final return to his possession. It remains true that the community of equals is a community of men. But, on the other hand, the text does not admit that landless rural workers exist, except as temporary victims of misfortune. Israelites are not to make slaves of such unfortunate fellow-Israelites, even if they are forced into dependency (vv. 39–43): thus the text makes it clear that they remain members of the community. Theologically, their equality is expressed in a different way: "they are my slaves whom I brought out of Egypt", says YHWH, and hence they should not be enslaved to others (vv. 42, 55); and if enslaved to a resident alien, they must be redeemed as soon as possible (vv. 47–52). As for urban residents, whose dwellings are not subject to restoration at the jubilee (vv. 29–30), it is clear that this rule only applies to residential property, not agricultural land. The assumption may well be that the resident, if an Israelite, will possess land either in the city's territory or elsewhere. (For this paragraph, see Houston 2006: 196–97.)

Therefore, within the limits that we shall explore below in relation to women, resident aliens and foreign slaves, this text does present the image of a community of equals. The remarkable thing is that it does so under social conditions which in many ways denied this ideal, and which it does not conceal. No hypotheses about the historical date and background of the Holiness Code are necessary to see that the author, or authors, were well aware of such social realities as the cash economy, the sale of land because of poverty, debt bondage and chattel slavery. Part of the object of the text seems to be to demonstrate that even under the conditions of the cash economy, where farmers may be threatened by bankruptcy and the loss of their land, it is still possible to maintain the old ideal of the community of equal "brothers".

Between jubilees, the maintenance of this ideal relies, in a similar way to Deut.15:7–11, on community feeling issuing in generosity towards the impoverished "brother". Of the lines of conduct urged in the four, successively more severe, cases of impoverishment in Lev. 25:23–55 the only one which could be said to be in the interest of the person addressed is the redemption of land; it would appear that there was no requirement to return the land to its original holder, the object being to retain it within the *mishpaha* (Milgrom 2000: 2195–96). In all the other cases the goodwill of the addressee is relied on, whether to give loans without interest, to maintain a worker in a state ambiguous as between debt bondage and wage labour, or to redeem a relative from slavery to a resident alien. But more problematic than any of these is the jubilee itself (vv. 8–19). No practical means of implementing it is suggested, and it could not be implemented unless the supposed initial conditions of a society without rich or poor had really existed. For example, the law includes the exhortation when buying and selling land, "do not take advantage of one another" (v. 14). But in reality it is only on one side that there could be any question of taking advantage. When the attachment of the peasant to the land is as strong as it was in ancient Israel and Judah, any sale must be a forced one. The buyer is in much the stronger position, and is able to force the price down. Because rich and poor do exist, because the society of the nation as a whole is stratified, a law like this will meet the entrenched refusal of the owners of capital to make it work.

Given this utopian character, it may be, and often is, questioned how valuable the text is as a challenge to justice in our day. The best way to answer this question is to trace the values which it presupposes (cf. Houston 2008: 200–02). The "community of equals", as I have called it, recalls modern (particularly American and French) concepts of democracy (cf. Dunn 2005: esp. 71–118). But there are significant differences. The text speaks explicitly of a proclamation of liberty (v. 8); and, as I have shown, it presupposes equality among its subjects. However, neither of these venerated ideals means the same thing in this text as it does in modern democratic societies. The meaning of equality in this text, as we have seen, is determined by the kinship-dominated communities from which it emerges: it is an equality of heads of family, and of their families only through their heads. Further, however, it implies among other things a rough (but not mathematical) equality of goods, whereas equality in modern Western democracies includes, besides the idea of equality before the law, the supposed equality of opportunity to acquire wealth, but definitely not equality of wealth. That is held to be liable to encroach on the other ideal of liberty, which is defined (as famously by J. S. Mill) as the freedom to do what I like (such as to acquire wealth) provided I do not infringe someone else's liberty. It is clear that "liberty" or *deror* in Lev. 25:8 means nothing like this, but rather being liberated from subservience to other humans to join, or rejoin, the community of equals, which has quite narrow restrictions on its freedom of action, especially in order to preserve its equality. In fact, the members of this liberated community are twice described as slaves! (vv. 42, 55) – of course the slaves of YHWH, just as their land, which the jubilee is to place them once more in possession of, is YHWH's land (v. 23), and they merely tenants. It could be said that the modern conception stresses liberty of action and the one in Leviticus liberty from enslavement; the modern one individual freedom and Leviticus the shared freedom of the liberated community.

I would judge that it is vitally important to reflect on the difference between these conceptions, while being clearly aware of the very different social configurations which have given birth to them. We should neither congratulate ourselves on our superiority to the ancients, nor confess that our divergence from the biblical concepts is in itself wrong – lines, as we have seen, taken by many today. This is fruitless, in view of the huge difference in our societies. It needs rather to be a question of dialogue. The inadequacies of the biblical ideas are immediately obvious to us. We have to work harder to see what may be lacking in our society and its controlling ideas, but it is obvious to many of us that it is idle to speak of equality where in Britain or the USA some CEOs are paid hundreds of times more than their least well-paid employees. The difference in power that this difference in income creates makes any talk of equality before the law or in electoral power meaningless; and "equality of opportunity" is a hollow slogan where the levers of opportunity – education, family support, decent housing – are also unfairly distributed.

Now clearly, to compare the stronger idea of equality in this text with this is to compare the reality of one society with the ideals of another, which is itself hardly fair. But reflection on the text may at least suggest why we are where we are and what might have to happen for us to get somewhere else. The point in my mind is that idea of liberty in Leviticus 25 as the *shared* freedom of a liberated *community*. Interestingly, while Sen discusses several different ideas of liberty (2009: 299–317), this shared liberty is not one of them: they are all individualist in one way or another. A sense of community, embracing the CEO and the cleaners, is what is manifestly lacking in our big companies, and equally so in the nation at large. It is not obvious how it could be created, short of a war against an invader. Equality is not the only loser.

We might indeed conclude that as a genuine community of equals is as unattainable in a modern capitalist democracy as it was in ancient Judah, it may nevertheless be attainable in a smaller group. This is what the monastic movement in Christian history has sometimes achieved, and one might mention also the co-operative movement or the original ideal of the Israeli kibbutzim. But of course, long before this, it was achieved or at least aimed at in the primitive Christian church. Before we go on to look at how the ideal is expressed in the New Testament, we should look carefully at those who can be seen to fall through the gaps in the community of equals in the Old Testament.

The Unequals

Women

It is flagrantly obvious that women are not considered equal to men in the Old Testament – even literally: Lev. 27:2–7 specifies the rates at which persons who have been dedicated to the sanctuary may be redeemed, an adult male at 50 shekels, an adult woman at 30. The frequent assertion that Gen. 1:27 makes male and female equal in that they are equally created in the image of God may be true as far as it goes, but there is no evidence that this was ever taken to mean that women should be treated equally or share the same tasks and authority as men (Clines 1990: 41–45). It is taken for granted throughout the Old Testament that public life is the sphere of men, and the domestic sphere belongs to women. This does not prevent Old Testament writers from creating pictures of strong, intelligent and ingenious women: one thinks of Rebekah, Tamar in Genesis 38, Abigail, and many others. But their ingenuity perhaps underlines the point: in order to get their way in a man's world, they must rely on their wits.

Women in the Civil Law. As we drew our picture of the community of
equals primarily from the laws of the Torah, we may illustrate the inequality
of women from the same source. Where there is no specific mention of
women, which is usual, the text may assume either that the case is one
where no woman would be involved (e.g. Exod. 21:18–19), or that if any is,
she should be treated in the same way as a man in the same position, for
example as the owner of a pit in Exod. 21:33–34.

Where women are mentioned, apart from the relatively few cases where
it is explicitly stated that the law applies to men and women equally (e.g.
Exod. 21:28; Deut. 15:17b), the case is usually a sexual one. Exodus 21:7–11
applies to a female slave used as a concubine. In this case the law which
applies to a male slave, that he should be released after six years' service,
does not apply, evidently because the woman would be unable to find any
kind of home or living as a cast-off concubine, except, no doubt, as a
prostitute. Exodus 22:16–17 concerns the seduction of an unmarried girl.[1]
A range of sexual behaviours, mostly incestuous, are prohibited in Lev.
18.6–23 and provided with penalties in Lev. 20.10–21: in all cases the
penalty is the same for the man and the woman, but there is seemingly no
recognition of the possibility of rape. This omission is repaired in Deut.
22:23–27, about sex between a betrothed girl and a man not her betrothed,
which is one of a range of sexual laws in Deut. 22:13–30; but though this
paragraph recognizes (by way of an example) the possibility that the girl
may not have agreed to sex, and therefore not be deserving of punishment,
it makes no difference to the guilt of the man, who dies in either case.
Presumably the law speaks of a betrothed virgin rather than a married
woman (cf. v. 22) on the assumption that a married woman would not be
found in the open country. Moreover, where the girl is not betrothed (Deut.
22:28–29, cf. Exod. 22:16–17), the possibility of rape is again not recognized,
since there is no punishment for the girl in any case; the man has to pay her
father compensation and must marry her (the latitude given to the father
in Exodus not to give the girl to her seducer or rapist seems to be withdrawn
in Deuteronomy). It even seems that a girl who has been raped must be the
one punished, by having to endure her rapist's attentions for the rest of

1. It is certain that in practically every case where the law speaks of a virgin or
a betrothed person, it is dealing with a person who would be regarded as a child
in modern Western legal systems: hence my use of "girl" is not intended to be
demeaning, but meant literally, to underline that the female is not an adult woman,
and that in our conception the man would be guilty of intercourse with a minor
in every case.

her life. Perhaps most unfair of all is the law on a newly-married man's accusation that his bride had not been a virgin (Deut. 22:13–19). If it is found that she was, he is to be flogged,[2] pay 100 shekels compensation to the family, and not be permitted to divorce her (the same problem for the woman!); if no evidence of her virginity is found, she is to be stoned to death. These provisions appear to contradict Deut. 19:16–20, which say that one who has given false evidence in favour of someone's conviction shall suffer the same punishment as the defendant would have suffered if found guilty.

Setting aside ritual law, which would raise a number of complex issues which there is no space to deal with here, the only other type of law where women are dealt with differently from men is the law of inheritance. It would appear from Num. 27:1–11 that at one time there was no possibility at all of women's inheriting. The law given by inspiration in reply to the request of the daughters of Zelophehad allows daughters to inherit where there are no sons, ahead of male relatives of the deceased. It is only in the case of a man having no sons that daughters can ever inherit, and other female relatives never. Even then, they are required to marry within the tribe (Numbers 36), so that property does not pass out of the tribal territories. The failure to mention the widow of a man leaving property has usually been taken as evidence, along with the vulnerable position of widows testified to elsewhere, that they were not provided for at all. However, counter-evidence should lead to caution about the "facts on the ground". Naomi appears to hold some property belonging to her dead husband (Ruth 4:3). But what one can say is that the ideal scheme as conceived by the priestly writer ignores any provision for the widow. This is entirely in line with the ideology elsewhere.

It must therefore be acknowledged that the civil law in the Torah is unfair to women; grossly unfair, one should say. To put it another way, justice is conceived in the Torah (and generally elsewhere in the Bible) in a way which does not take account of women, and when, as with sexual offences, it is necessary to mention women, they are treated in a way which takes account largely only of the interests of the family, which is defined by the male line and therefore constituted by its male members. In the case of false accusation, the man has impugned the honour of his bride's family through her, and therefore has to compensate them; but if the accusation is found to be true her family's honour is more gravely besmirched by the

2. Assuming this is what *weyisseru oto* means; NRSV, REB "punish him", which seems redundant.

reality than it could be by an accusation, and so is that of the family of the bridegroom: hence the death penalty for the erring woman. The failure to recognize rape as increasing the guilt of a man's forbidden liaison, or at all where the woman is not forbidden to him for marriage, is in line with the same ideology of honour. Family honour is damaged by a woman losing her virginity, unless this is covered by an appropriate compensation (not just for bridal payment forgone). Whether she took part willingly or was forced does not affect this issue, though it may affect her own guilt.

The conclusion is that it is all very well for a conservative interpreter like Wright to point out that families are included in the community of equals through their heads. In ordinary conditions they were under the protection of the family head; but once a rift or a point of conflict develops within a family, it rapidly becomes clear that the equality of families is of no benefit to those who are not its head. Even adult male sons of living parents are clearly subordinate to their parents (including the mother) in the law: Exod. 21:15 prescribes the death penalty for one who strikes a parent, and Deut. 21:18–23 for an insubordinate and profligate son. The law says little about minors below the age of betrothal, but it is clear that they had little protection from whatever their father chose to do with them: we know from the texts in 2 Kings and Nehemiah quoted earlier that they were frequently offered as collateral for loans. Moreover, widows and orphans, who had lost their male protector, were dangerously open to exploitation by the head of the *bet ab* or by others (Bendor 1996: 190–94). They then had to rely on the narrative of justice discussed in the previous chapter, that is on the freely chosen generosity of a patron.

Aliens and foreign slaves
This is true even more of the *ger*, the person resident in a community who originates from outside it and has no stake in it, as illustrated by the very frequent exhortations in the Torah not to oppress the *ger*. Originally anyone from another village or *mishpaha*, let alone another tribe or nation, anyone who did not possess a landholding in the community, would probably have been regarded as a *ger* (Weber 1952: 28–33; Rogerson 2009: 189, n. 50), and this broad definition may apply in a few texts. But in most places in the Torah as we have it, the *ger* is a person resident among Israel who is not by descent a member of the people. This meaning is obvious in e.g. Deut. 14:21, and therefore no doubt in Deuteronomy as whole; or in the Holiness Code, which often specifies that its laws apply equally to natives and *gerim* (e.g. Lev. 17:8; 18:26; 20:2). The lack of a stake in the land laid the *ger* open to abuse.

While exhortations not to oppress the alien are frequent in most parts of the Torah, oppression is not defined. Is the permission given in Lev. 25:44–46 to acquire slaves both from neighbouring nations and from "the settlers who reside among you, and from their family whom they give birth to in your land"[3] not oppression? With the explicit permission given in v. 46 to pass on such slaves by inheritance, and the inexplicit but unmistakable permission to work them hard, the difference from what Israelites have a right to expect is very clear. Yet earlier in the same legal collection, we have the most powerful statement, though legally unenforceable, that they should be treated in exactly the same way as Israelites. Lev. 19:34 inserts between two clauses very similar to Exod. 22:21 this exhortation: "The stranger who resides with you shall be like the native: you shall love him as yourself", which of course recalls, and is intended to recall, Lev. 19:18 in an earlier part of the same chapter, "You shall love your neighbour as yourself". Verses 18 and 34 taken together imply that the *ger* is a neighbour. The parable of the good Samaritan simply puts into story form this neat answer to the scribe's question, "Who is my neighbour?" This verse, if no other, suggests that the *ger* is in a certain sense a member of the community of equals, since "neighbour" defines such a member in other places.

It is clear enough that the community of Israel, perhaps especially in the Second Temple period, struggled with ambiguous feelings in relation to the many people of other ethnicities who lived among them. On the one hand, the community was primarily defined in terms of kinship (real or fictive); it was a community of "brothers". On the other, it was felt that everyone resident in the community deserved protection from exploitation, and that led to the alien becoming a de facto member of the community. It is obvious that this ambiguity was in many ways no different from that presented by our own community, where the belief that migrants need their human rights protected struggles with tabloid xenophobia.

We have seen that the ideal commended by the Torah in relation to what is called "slavery" of Israelites is that this is a time-limited contract of labour service undertaken, we presume, to pay off a debt, though this is not actually said in the passages concerned with it (Exod. 21:2–6; Deut. 15:12–18). On the other hand, Lev. 25:44–46 is very explicit that foreigners may be bought as chattel slaves, without hope of redemption. Prisoners of war, whether military or civilian, were normally enslaved in the ancient

3. The word *ger* is not used, but the verbal designation "who reside" (*haggarim*) is derived from the same root, and the phrase is explicit enough to make it clear that that is who is meant.

world, and Deut. 20:14 permits this practice, while v. 11, slightly differently, refers to forced labour, in effect state slavery.

Even setting aside time-limited debt-bondage, there is no one way to characterize slavery in the ancient world. The type most familiar to us in modern history, the mass plantation slavery of persons transported from Africa to the Americas and their descendants, has only limited parallels in the ancient world: the closest parallel is the gangs of slaves which worked large estates in Roman times. But these, typical of Italy and Sicily, probably did not exist in the East, though mines in Greece were often worked by slaves. Romans also had domestic slaves who were normally freed at the owner's will while still able to make a living for themselves, or bought their own freedom by saving the monetary allowance made to them. Greek slaves were less often freed. We do not have enough information to enable us to fit chattel slavery in Israel and Judah into the spectrum, but there is no question that it existed.

We have to conclude that the concept of the community of equals in ancient Israel and Judah had limitations, and these limitations are inherent rather than accidental to the concept as developed. For the concept is an outgrowth of a particular social formation, and shares in that formation's strengths and weaknesses. Its main strength is the wholeness of its vision of equality, which is not limited to formal, legal or political equality; its weaknesses are that it is based on a group bound (supposedly) by kinship, and exclusive of people not seen as sharing that bond.

The community of the primitive Church

Does the early Church overcome the drawbacks of the community of equals as conceived in the Old Testament documents? The "egalitarian impulses" in the Pauline communities are discussed by David Horrell (2005: 99–132), who argues that they do not necessarily imply actual equality and are balanced by Paul's assertion of his own authority – but that is often exercised on behalf of the disadvantaged and against arrogant self-assertion within the Christian community (ib.: 118). At bottom, the key requirement is not so much equality as unity, unity in Christ.

Paul (and other early Christian writers, e.g. Heb. 3:1, Jas 1:2) addresses Christian congregations as "brothers" (*adelphoi*, NRSV "brothers and sisters", REB "my friends"). The word in this case clearly covers both sexes, and is also used in the singular to mean what is meant today by "a (fellow) Christian" (e.g. Rom. 14:10; the feminine is used when appropriate, e.g. 1 Cor. 9:5). It has been pointed out that this is much the commonest term used for "Christians" in Paul (see Horrell 2005: 111).

It might be described as a purely conventional usage for members of a close-knit society, but there is more to it than that. For Paul bases his arguments about accepting one another's peculiarities in things indifferent, particularly diet, in part on the idea of brotherhood (Horrell 2005:110–15; cf. Horrell 2001). Note the number of times the word *adelphos* is used in Rom. 14: vv. 10 (twice), 13, 15, 21 (NRSV usually "brother or sister", REB "fellow-Christian"). At Rom. 14:15, for example: "For if your brother (or sister) is pained by what you eat, you are no longer behaving in love. Do not destroy one for whom Christ died by what you eat." A similar point is made in 1 Corinthians 8: "Your 'knowledge' destroys the 'weak' person, who is a brother or sister for whom Christ died" (v. 11). Paul himself agrees in principle with the "strong" who believe it is permissible to eat meat sacrificed to idols (or, in Romans, food unclean according to the Mosaic law); hence the words "strong" and "weak" do express his own assessment of the strength of faith of the different groups. In that respect the individuals are not equal (Dunn 1988: 812). Nevertheless, they are to be treated as if equal. Christ died for all of them, and the consciences of the "weak" are to be respected as much as those of the strong.

A similar idea informs the parable of the body and its parts in 1 Cor. 12:12–27. It is true that this image is a commonplace which in its next most well-known usage was not used to preach an idea of equality: in the speech of Menenius Agrippa in Livy, it is used to induce the plebs, who are on strike, to return to their responsibilities and accept their inferior position. But in the way it is developed in Paul, it makes a plainly egalitarian point: "God has arranged the body, giving peculiar honour to the inferior parts"; that is, when a part of the body falls short of the others, that is the part which is honoured – a different procedure to what we are used to, where reward, honour, prizes, are given to those who are superior to others in any case. Thus Paul urges the more spiritually "advanced" Corinthians not to despise those who do not display the more showy charismatic gifts.

The word "equality" (*isotes*) itself is used by Paul in his discussion of the collection for the poor of the Jerusalem church in 2 Cor. 8 (vv. 13–14). Horrell notes, however, that in Greek thought this is "not … equivalent to the modern notion of equality … but conveyed the sense of 'proper balance' or 'fairness' (cf. Col. 4.1)" (Horrell 2005: 239). But in this context it clearly refers to "a kind of mutualism" of reciprocal giving (v. 14; Horrell 2005: ib.). This giving of reciprocal gifts to help each other's need is the model of giving typical of egalitarian communities, and is not related to patronage.

In Paul's exhortation it is urged as the example given by Christ (v. 9), "that you through his poverty might become rich".

Luke idealizes this characterization of the Christian community – in Paul a goal to be striven for rather than a reality – in his portrait of the early Jerusalem church, Acts 4:32–37, with its sharing of material goods in common: "No one regarded any of their possessions as their own, but they were all shared in common." This is a more radical equality than is to be found elsewhere, but Luke may well be generalizing from Barnabas's action (and the story of Ananias and Sapphira), and failing to distinguish between *selling* property for the benefit of the community and putting property into common possession (Haenchen 1971: 231–33).

However that may be, it is clear that the community of equals here does indeed leap over many of the differences which stand out in the Old Testament concept. The founding presupposition of the Gentile church is the equality of Jews and Gentiles. The community includes women and men on equal terms so far as their participation in the community is concerned: so women exercise all the spiritual gifts, including prophecy (1 Cor. 11:5) and apostleship (Junia in Rom. 16:7 – not to be read "Junias"! (see Dunn 1988: 894)). Many Christians are slaves, but they too within the body of the Church are equal. Paul expresses this in the famous epigram of Gal. 3: 28, "There is here [in Christ] no Jew or Greek, no slave or free, no male and female; for you are all one in Christ Jesus."

We ought to be careful to see how this statement of oneness in Christ differs from a modern idea of "human rights", rights which inhere in a person because she or he is a human being without any distinction of gender, class, or nationality or race (see Sen 2009: 355–87 for a discussion of human rights in the modern context). In the first place it describes the body of Christ: it is not a general statement about humanity as such. However, it does surely imply that the call to put one's faith in Christ is one which comes to all without distinction. Second, it is not about equality but about unity: "you are all one", there are no distinctions. Third, it does not concern rights but privileges: "You are all children of God through faith in Christ Jesus" (v. 26). In other words, the community of equals which is the Christian church has no distinctions within it, but its external boundaries are defined by faith. It is also clear that within a couple of generations, at latest, traditional distinctions had reasserted themselves: thus the post-Pauline writer who composed 1 Timothy puts women in their place within the Church as well as in the home (1 Tim. 2:8–15; the following passage, 3:1–13, appears to restrict the office of bishop to men, and probably also that of deacon).

We should also recognize that the full implications of this unity are not drawn in the New Testament itself, or indeed for many centuries afterwards. Although men and women, slave and free, participate in Christ on equal terms, the New Testament contains a number of passages (the so-called "household tables") giving instruction on how Christians are to conduct themselves in various relations of life, and in all cases the conventional understanding of those relations is upheld. The principal passages are Eph. 5:21–6:9; Col. 3:18–4:1; 1 Pet. 2:18–3:7. It is likely that they derive from a time somewhat later than that of Paul, but they no doubt represent his views. Wives are to be subordinate to husbands, slaves are to obey their owners, even when treated unjustly (1 Pet. 2:18); and Christological teaching is given to support these instructions.

It is not surprising that Christian slave-owners right into the modern era were able to defend slavery on biblical grounds. However, the fact that New Testament writers do not urge Christian slave-owners to free their slaves should not be seen as a culpable failure to draw the implications of unity in Christ, as is done by Margaret Davies (1995). There were legal restrictions on the right of owners to manumit their slaves (Meggitt 1998: 181–82). Paul urges Philemon to receive Onesimus back as a "brother" rather than as a slave. The relationship is more important than the legality. Onesimus will still be a slave, but it is more significant that he will be "a beloved brother" (Phlm. 16). The teaching of "all one in Christ", if taken in full seriousness, carries the implication that people should be treated equally in a practical way. It is not simply a theological idea. If a slave, or a wage slave for that matter, is a brother or sister, I should treat him or her as such, which means not profiting from their suffering. But if that applies to brothers and sisters in Christ, it must surely apply to everybody.

Chapter 6

THE STORY OF JESUS: JUSTICE IN PRACTICE

We have already referred on a number of occasions to aspects of Jesus' teaching which express distinctive understandings of the justice of God (above, pp. 44–45, 49–50). In this chapter I want rather to present the story of Jesus as justice – God's justice – expressed in practice. But which story? There are four canonical Gospels, each telling the story in its own way. There are many retellings of the Gospel which attempt to weave material from all four into a single narrative, not only in modern times but going back to Tatian in the second century. There have also been numerous attempts by modern scholars to reconstruct the story of the historical Jesus by distinguishing in the Gospels between "authentic" and "secondary" material. The object of this book is to focus on what is said *in the Bible* about our subject, so it is right that we should set on one side all these reconstructions and harmonizations, illuminating as they may sometimes be, and take up one of the canonical Gospels as our source, without trying to determine how much of it may be historically "authentic". For each of the Gospels gives an authentic picture of how Jesus was viewed by someone, or some community, in the early Church.

Which Gospel shall we use? It would be possible to use any of them, but here I shall use Mark, for a number of reasons: because it is the shortest; because it is generally regarded as Matthew and Luke's principal source, while John may have used one or more of the three Synoptic Gospels as a source; because I have already used material distinctive to Matthew and Luke above; and because it is manifestly concerned with the authority of Jesus as set against other authorities in society, and authority is a matter closely connected with justice. Mark as a political text has been especially explored by Ched Myers in his remarkable book *Binding the Strong Man* (1988). The signs are evident that the Gospel was composed in a situation where the infant church was facing persecution from the state. This is explicit in Mk 13:9–13, "you shall stand before governors and kings for my sake", and clearly implied in such key texts as 8:34–38, "take up your cross and follow me", and 10:39, "You (James and John) shall drink the cup that I drink".

We shall discover as we move through the Gospel that all three of the narratives of justice we have looked at are taken up, but combined with each other in ways which result in an entirely new and creative practice. The question of authority is of course related in the first place to justice as cosmic order, as we have seen in Chapter 3. Jesus as the Son of God has authority over the "unclean spirits" (Mk 1:27). Jesus' exorcisms are the leading example of his authority in Mark's Gospel. As he says in 3:23–27, they are the sign that Satan's kingdom over this world is at an end – and hence, though this is not explicit in this episode in Mark (cf. Matt. 12:28; Lk 11:20), that God's kingdom is inaugurated. This is a challenge to all unjust systems of human rule, though I cannot follow Myers (1988: 146–49) in interpreting the exorcisms as political symbolic actions. Myers's examples of Luther nailing up his 95 theses and Martin Luther King praying in the face of police violence are beside the point. Rather, the Gospel identifies the demons and the scribal authorities (with Herod and the Romans) as independent opponents of divine rule who each oppress God's people in their own way. Between these parallel struggles there are echoes rather than a consistent system of symbolism, even if symbolism is apparent in an individual episode, the exorcism of "Legion" (Mk 5.1–20). It is reasonable, however, to ask how Mark understands the outlines of the *justice* proclaimed by the authority of Jesus.

Jesus' authority is announced right at the beginning of the Gospel by the divine voice at his baptism, "You are my beloved son; I delight in you" (1:11). There is a clear reference here to Ps. 2:7, where YHWH addresses the Davidic king, "You are my son; today I have begotten you", and also to Isa. 42:1, "Here is my servant … my chosen one, in whom I delight". Jesus is thus identified as the one who bears God's authority to bring justice on earth (Pss. 72; 101; Isa. 42:1–4). This is shortly followed by Mark's summary of his preaching, "The time is fulfilled and the kingdom of God has drawn near; repent, and believe the good news" (1:15). We have again seen, in the Psalms, that the announcement of the reign of God is closely linked to his "coming to judge the earth", to restore justice and righteousness (Pss. 96; 98). It is easy to see that Mark intends us to understand that this reign of justice is to be inaugurated by Jesus.

It is with the series of confrontations in 2:1–3:6 that the question of authority begins to be disputed with Jewish authorities, variously described as "scribes", "scribes of the Pharisees" and "Pharisees". The latter are said in 3:6 to conspire with the Herodians, i.e. the supporters of the Herod family, and in particular of Antipas, ruler of Galilee, to destroy Jesus. The confrontation is resumed with "the Pharisees and some of the scribes" in 3:20–29 and 7:1–13, and on these occasions Mark says that they have come from Jerusalem (3:22; 7:1); that is to say, they represent the authorities of what Myers calls the "temple-state" (1988: 166). Inevitably, from the moment of Jesus' symbolic entry as Messiah into Jerusalem (11:1–11), the confrontation is continuous, and now the "chief priests" (11:18, etc.) and the "elders" (11:27, etc.), that is to say the leading members of the ruling class, priestly and lay, are drawn into the struggle. Thus Jesus' opponents are not simply religious authorities. Even to the Romans, often believed to be the chief persecutors in Mark's own day, "illicit cults" were a political matter, threatening the authority of the state. But in any case the political message of the triumphal entry, 11:1–11, and the parable of the tenants, 12:1–12, is unmistakable. Jesus enters Jerusalem as Messiah, that is, its legitimate ruler, and denounces the existing authorities for rejecting the messengers of God, ultimately the Messiah, God's own Son (see below).

But it is the content of the disputes that lets us into the character and meaning of the kingdom of God, the nature of God's justice as proclaimed by his Messiah. In the first, in 2:1–12, Jesus tells the paralytic, "Your sins are forgiven". The scribes who are sitting there object silently that this is blasphemy. Only God can forgive sins. Who could disagree with that? – but sins were in fact regularly forgiven in the temple system, so the real question must be who is entitled to represent God's authority: the temple system, or Jesus (Myers 1988: 155). Jesus then demonstrates that he represents the power of the one who can kill or make alive by saying to the paralytic, "Take up your bed and walk", which he does, to the amazement of all present.

The point that God's kingdom means the forgiveness of sins is underlined in a different way in the following episode (2:13–17), in which Jesus calls Levi, a customs collector, to follow him, and proceeds to eat with him and other customs collectors and "sinners". "The scribes of the Pharisees" object to this. The point is that the collectors of tolls on produce entering towns were believed to be corrupt as a body. The system of bidding for the contract encouraged profiteering by the contractors, and their employees took as much as they could as it passed through their hands (Jeremias 1969: 310). The objection to them is not, as sometimes thought, that they were quislings; but clearly the corruption is part of the unjust political system under Antipas and the Romans, and its effect compounds the injustice. Respectable people would have nothing to do with them socially. E. P. Sanders argues that Jesus called sinners such as customs collectors, that is wicked and unjust people, not just people who were technically in breach of the law, to follow him *unconditionally*, that is without demanding that they should repent (Sanders 1985: 200–08). Sanders is attempting to reconstruct the life of the historical Jesus. But the point is tolerably clear even in Mark's narrative. Jesus' unconditional association with people who were known in general to be corrupt, and his defence, "I have not come to invite just people but sinners" (2:17), inaugurates a totally new approach to the battle with injustice. It is undermined from within by inviting the unjust into the transforming company of the Son of God.

It thus becomes evident that the character of God's justice in the reign of God announced by Jesus participates also in the second of our narratives of justice, on justice as faithfulness. God's faithful saving power is not exercised impartially, but with a preferential option for sinners. It is sinners to whom God through Jesus becomes committed. The Pauline doctrine that all are sinners is not relevant here. Sinners are a defined group in the social context sketched by Mark, and it is these who are sought out by Jesus. It is clear, however, from other narratives that this is not an exclusive option. The saving practice of Jesus as a whole is directed towards the needy of all kinds, the sick, the possessed, the disabled and the poor.

This is evident in the following three clashes, about fasting (2:18–22) and the sabbath (2:23–3:6). The issue of the sabbath, in view of Num. 15:32–36, was potentially a matter for the courts. The issue is whether the observance of an institution intended to forward justice (Deut. 5:15) should be governed by rules ("Why are they doing what is forbidden on the sabbath?", Mk 2:24), or by the needs of human beings. "The sabbath came into existence for human beings, not human beings for the sabbath" (2:27). Because Jesus, as Messiah, is "lord also of the sabbath" (2:28), he is able to authorize a just and life-giving (3:4) observance of it.

The dispute about eating with unwashed hands (7:1–13) follows similar lines, but it concerns not the written Torah but a tradition, one of the Pharisees' traditions, according to Mark. (Mark reflects Jewish practice of his own time, rather than that of Jesus, in saying that "all the Jews" wash before eating, 7:3 (cf. Sanders 1985: 185–86).) Jesus accuses the Pharisees of nullifying the Torah with their traditions. Yet Mark interprets him (probably[1]) as subsequently revoking observance of all the food laws (7.19b), which of course were part of the Torah. Jesus is not likely to have intended

---

1. But Mk 7:19b may mean only that he declared clean all foods permitted by the Torah (Crossley 2009).

this, but Mark presents him as sovereign even over the Torah itself, in this case setting aside the main obstacle to table-fellowship between Jewish and Gentile Christians (cf. Acts 10). The point is underlined by the following episode (7:24–30) of the Gentile woman with her repartee about the crumbs from the children's table. The ultimate meaning of Jesus' teaching, as Mark understands it, thus includes the creation of a community of equals, here between Jews and Gentiles. We shall return to this point shortly.

Returning to ch. 3, the next dispute, with scribes from Jerusalem, concerns the power by which Jesus performs exorcisms: "he casts out demons by the power of the ruler of the demons" (3:22). Rather than a genuine dispute, this appears to be a confected accusation designed to cause trouble. Yet Jesus takes it seriously and shows the absurdity of the idea (vv. 23–26), before making the positive point (v. 27) that successful exorcisms imply that Satan's power has been bound by God's power in him. However, what is told here is no mere power struggle, even on the lines of the Egyptian plagues: for the actual exorcisms are carried out in compassion for human beings who have fallen under the power of the demons. This becomes clear in the story, which shortly follows, of the possessed man of the Gentile city Gerasa, which is told at length (5:1–20), and ends with Jesus' command, different from the commands to secrecy given in Jewish country, "Go back to your home and to your people, and report to them all that the Lord has done for you in mercy." Here the name Legion which the demons give to themselves may seem to give some support to Myers' view of the exorcisms as political symbolism. The same power over the demons is given to the Twelve in their mission (6:7), which they carry out in the name of Jesus (one can assume this, and it is implied in 9:38). Jesus' authority is shown to extend further, to the natural elements, in the stilling of the storm (4:35–41) and his walking on the water (6:45–52) and in the feeding miracles (6:30–44, 8:1–9).

In the second half of the Gospel, from 8:27, Jesus begins to teach his disciples about the fate that awaits him – and them. First he elicits from Peter the recognition that he is the Messiah (8:29), which means that this fate is inexplicable in traditional theological terms, as Peter perceives (v. 32). There were other claimants to Messiahship, and each of them eventually was defeated by the Romans, and if not killed in battle would be crucified; and in each case that was the end of the Messianic claim. Against this background it is truly extraordinary that Mark's Jesus is able to forecast that fate in advance and still accept recognition as Messiah. It is only explained by the little phrase "and rise after three days" at the end of v. 31. This is for Mark the ground on which he can present Jesus to his own readers as the living Messiah, the authority over their lives, the preacher of God's just rule. And he is clear that Jesus asks his followers to be prepared to share his fate: "If you wish to come after me, you must deny yourself and take up your cross and follow me. For if you wish to save your life you will lose it, and if you lose your life for the sake of the Gospel, you will save it" (8:34–35, second person substituted for the third). "For the sake of the Gospel" implies that the threat of martyrdom faces those in particular who were sent out as missionaries like the Twelve. The transfiguration (9:2–8) confirms God's approval of God's son, and God uses similar words to those at the baptism (v. 7), but with the significant addition "listen to him", and of course in totally changed circumstances. Since then Jesus has come to grips with the powers that now control God's people, and they are closing in. The transfiguration thus also foreshadows the resurrection in visible form.

But the fate of the Messiah has also significant implications for the character of his practice of justice, as soon becomes clear. Each of the two further predictions of the passion is followed by a passage on the need for humility, and at this point in the Gospel we begin to hear language implying that the kingdom of God is not simply the reign of God but is a realm that can be "entered" or a rule that can be "accepted" (9:47; 10:14–15, 23–25; 12:34; 14:25). To do so requires humility, a commitment to renounce the domination of others. In other words, the kingdom of God as Mark's Jesus sees it is a community of equals, under God. Authority can only be exercised for the sake of justice within that limitation.

The Son of Man is to be handed over into the hands of human beings (9:31); the disciples must learn to be the last of all and the servant of all. They need to learn to accept the kingdom of God as children (9:33–37). The Son of Man is to be handed over to the Gentiles (10:33); the disciples need to learn how different the kingdom of God is from the kingdom of the Gentiles. James and John want the foremost places in Jesus' glory, very likely for the sake of power (de Mingo 2003: 102). But to share his fate is the closest they will get. De Mingo strikingly suggests that those for whom places on Jesus' right and left "are prepared" are the bandits crucified with him (15:27; de Mingo 2003: 114). The exchange prompts Jesus to spell out the difference between worldly rule and his own community. "Those who are supposed to rule the Gentiles lord it over them, and their great ones make them feel the weight of their authority. But it is not so among you. Whoever wishes to be great among you will be your servant, and whoever wishes to be first among you will be the slave of all" (10:42–44). This is a profound transformation of values, considering the degraded condition of the slave in ancient society. The rejection of domination could not be more strongly expressed. But the disciples can go this way because the master has trodden it. "For the Son of man did not come to be served but to serve, and to give his life a ransom for many" (10:45).

Between these two blocks of teaching is placed the highly elaborated episode of the rich man who seeks Jesus' advice on gaining eternal life (10:17–31). A different aspect of renunciation is in view here. One notes the difference between the unconditional call extended to Levi, the doubtless corrupt and possibly rich tax collector, and the condition – "sell all you have and give to the poor" – set on the call to follow Jesus to this man, who claims to have observed the commandments since his youth. It is customary for commentators and preachers to observe that the man's riches formed an obstacle, even an idol (Cranfield 1963: 330), keeping him from God. But the greatest difference between him and Levi is that while both have lived at the expense of others, Levi would not have claimed to have kept the commandments. Yet the reason why it was difficult for a rich person to enter the kingdom of God was because it was (and is) difficult to be rich without breaking at least one of the commandments. It is striking that the tenth commandment should be quoted in the form "do not defraud", or "deprive someone of what is due to them". This sharpens its relevance to the social conditions in view here, in which the owners of property live at the expense of those who contribute to their rent roll (Myers 1988: 272). Before he can make any progress, the man has to realize what Levi knew only too well, that his wealth in truth belongs to others. The kingdom of God is a community of equals. It has no room for those who dominate, whether by riches, or force, or attributed position. Yet Jesus is said to have "loved" the man (v. 21). For this man is a sinner, and yet pitiably unaware of it! The rich are inescapably sinners: that is the message of the episode and it is that that amazes the disciples (v. 26; cf. Crossley 2005); and, as we have already seen, it is sinners that Jesus has come to call. But the call must involve repentance for those who like this man do not yet recognize their sin.

Jesus' exercise of authority in service and the giving of his life is the most profound reversal of normal expectations in the Gospel. It may be regarded as the final theological statement of Jesus' significance before the passion narrative begins with the account of the triumphal entry. It is not entirely unexpected within the context of Mark, however, for, as we have seen, at each of the points where a clash of authority has occurred, it has been made clear that Jesus' authority as Messiah is exercised on the side of human need.

Jesus, who has, one must presume, made his way on foot hitherto, enters Jerusalem on the back of a colt, clearly with set intent. There can be little doubt Mark intends an allusion to Zech. 9:9 (LXX), where Zion's king comes to her "just and a saviour, humble and riding on an ass and a young colt". It is not quite clear in Mark that it is a donkey's colt, but in view of the text as it stands in the Septuagint of Zechariah, this does not matter. He is hailed by his followers in a manner which hints at his Messiahship, even if it does not state it explicitly (11:9–10, quoting Ps. 118:25–26; Taylor 1952: 452). Taken together, the action of Jesus and that of the crowd imply that Jesus is Messiah, but define his Messiahship as a practice of saving justice exercised in humility.

His "cleansing of the Temple" (11:15–18) is an open, though symbolic, exercise of Messianic authority – in the kingdom of Judah the king was responsible for the Temple and its worship. But more significantly for our purpose, it is a protest against the economic exploitation of the poor represented by the temple and its commercial activities, which as Myers points out, were an integral part of its work, and a source of profit for its authorities (Myers 1988: 300). Jesus' quotation of Isa. 56:7 points to the true function of the temple, to gather an inclusive community; while that of Jer. 7:11 threatens its destruction (Myers 1988: 303). The Temple authorities respond to this frontal assault as expected (11:18).

The following day they openly raise with Jesus the question of his authority (11:27–28). Jesus' reply (11:29–33) is more than a neat evasion. By posing the alternatives of divine and human authority for John's baptizing activity, he points to the reality of his own divine authority. The parable of the vineyard and its tenants continues the argument (12:1–12). Its meaning in the context is transparent. The authorities refuse to recognize the authority of God as exercised through God's prophets, such as John; in the end they will kill God's own son, "the heir", to whom they owe obedience, and the result, for them, will be disaster. The question about paying the poll tax to the imperial power (12:13–17) is a good response from the Pharisees and Herodians. Not only because any yes-or-no answer will expose Jesus to the danger either of action from the authorities or the loss of his popular support (Myers 1988: 310), but because one responsible for the just rule of God's people must be concerned about this impost of a thoroughly unjust system. Jesus' answer is a statement of formal justice: "to each his own": but of course it is not too difficult to apply the consideration that "what belongs to God" is everything – "The earth is the Lord's and all that is therein" (Ps. 24:1), which undermines the superficial impression that Caesar is owed anything (cf. Myers 1988:

310–14). Perhaps, though, the practical implication is that the tax may be paid, but as a matter of prudence, to avoid angering the authorities, not as a duty (cf. Matt. 17.24–27).

If most of these two chapters seems to be concerned with the formal issue of authority, they conclude with two paragraphs which address the use of authority and the content of justice. The denunciation of the scribes in 12:38–40 makes it clear that the current authorities exercise authority in the way identified as Gentile in 10:42, for their own honour and acquisition of wealth. It has already been made clear that this is not the way of the messianic kingdom. The passage about the widow's offering in 12:41–44 has been variously interpreted. Most frequently it is assumed that the widow offers a moral example in her total devotion to God (recently reaffirmed by Boring (2006: 352) in opposition to the view taken here), and a contrast to the rich man of ch. 10. There are several reasons why this is unconvincing (see Myers (1988: 321–22), who cites Wright 1982). First, Jesus utters no word of commendation: he simply states the objective fact that she has put in her last penny. Second, the object of her charity, the Temple, cannot be ignored; and Jesus has been in conflict with the Temple authorities, and is about to tell his disciples that the day is coming when not one stone of it will be left upon another (13:2). Third, he has just mentioned that the scribes "consume widows' households" (12:40). But he does not condemn her either. Her motives are pure, but she has been misdirected by the ruling figures of her nation, and deprived of "her whole livelihood". Just rule would ensure that the service of God was maintained by God's people in proportion to their means, and that the poor were not exploited in the name of God.

It is clear that this just rule, the kingdom of God, the rule of God's Messiah, is not in effect at this moment, neither at the time when Jesus faces arrest and crucifixion, nor the time of Mark, nor indeed that of any subsequent reader. The text must face this fact: hence ch. 13, in which Jesus warns against apocalyptic excitement (vv. 3–8), and of the persecution that Christians must expect in the coming time (9–13), before the great tribulation: the language of vv. 14–22 hints at the war against the Romans which is to end in such disaster. It is only after all this that the final victory may be expected (vv. 24–27).

This is the immediate prologue to the account of the final days of Jesus' earthly life, in which his enemies finally overtake him and hand him over to the Gentile power. The account includes one major statement by Jesus interpreting his death. This is of course 14:22–25, the words over the bread and cup. Here he says that his blood is to be "poured out for many" as the sealing of a covenant. This needs to be taken together with 10:45, "and give his life a ransom for many". However it is interpreted, what is clear is that his death is not simply an unlucky accident to be reversed by resurrection and second coming, but has a meaning in itself. His life is to be given "for many", a word with broad implications, since the gospel is to be preached throughout the world (13:10; 14:9). Nevertheless, the probably sacrificial language of 14:22, 25 points back to the statement that Jesus has "come to invite ... sinners". Jesus' death is God's saving power for his own favoured ones, the sinners he came to call to his table.

Jesus' confession before the High Priest, "I am [the Messiah], and you will see the Son of man sitting at the right hand of the Power, and coming with the clouds of heaven" (14:62), tells the readers of the Gospel nothing that they do not already know; however, its clear allusion to Ps. 110:1 as well as to Dan. 7:13, already alluded to in 13:26, is a plain reference to a text that would be taken as Messianic, and which Jesus has already discussed as such in his teaching (12:35–37). It begins a chain of scriptural allusions that appear especially in the account of the crucifixion. Mark 15:24 refers to Ps. 22:18, Mk 15:29 to v. 7 of the same psalm, and Jesus' cry of dereliction "My God, my God, why have you forsaken me?" quotes the first verse of the psalm; while 15:36 alludes to Ps. 69:21. The effect of these references is to indicate that the death of the Messiah was foreshadowed in Scripture. Since Psalm 22 and Psalm 69 both turn from lament to praise of God's salvation, they would also be read as pointing to the resurrection. Both crucifixion and resurrection are therefore part of God's plan.

The authentic text of Mark's Gospel is generally agreed to end at 16:8, and has been filled out by later hands. It is not known whether that is all he wrote, or whether his original ending has been lost. At all events, the announcement "He goes before you into Galilee" (16:7) makes a suitably dramatic ending as the book stands. As in his earthly life, Jesus continues to lead his followers, always going before them to gather the poor and the sinners into his kingdom.

Reflection

I began by suggesting that the focus of Mark's Gospel on the authority of Jesus makes it a suitable vehicle for reflection on the justice of God within the messianic community, in that the purpose of authority is to exercise justice. But we have seen that the narrative of justice as cosmic order, justice expressed in the authoritative activity of a king or the authoritative word of a prophet, is not adequate to express Jesus' practice of justice in Mark. It is simultaneously loving and saving power directed towards the needy and the sinners, and above all the gathering of a community of equals in mutual service. Mark 10:45 sums it up perfectly: "The Son of Man came not to be served but to serve, and to give his life a ransom for many."

His justice, the service of his people, has been exercised on the side of human need and against arbitrary rules, against Satanic power and on the side of those trapped by it, on the side of forgiveness and inclusion and against retribution and exclusion. He has worked tirelessly for the real needs of the humble people of Galilee, and defended them against those who would have used them as bricks and mortar for their great erections of political or religious power. In the context of our study in this book, we can see that Mark's Jesus indeed fulfils the terms of the Psalm's evocation of the ideal Davidic king, who "has pity on the poor and the needy, and saves the lives of the needy" (Ps. 72.13), but in a way probably not envisaged by the author of that Psalm, who would have thought only of top-down justice, rather than of one who works among and as one of the people whom he serves.

Still less would that author have envisaged a *crucified* king, one who is rejected by the temporary authorities of his own people in the service of a foreign power and suffers the humiliating death of a criminal slave. We have not only Paul's word for it that "a crucified Messiah [is] a stumbling-block to the Jews and foolishness to the Gentiles" (1 Cor. 1:23). There is a graffito at Rome in which a man stands with a raised hand before a crudely drawn human figure on a cross; the figure has a donkey's head, and the caption appears to mean "Alexamenos worships [his] god" (Alexamenos graffito 2009). The implication is that to worship a crucified man is like worshipping a donkey. But the crucified Messiah, the crucifixion of the Messiah and the Messiahship of the crucified one, is boldly affirmed by Mark, who presents Jesus as giving his death meaning, as the gift of life to the "many". While what passes for justice in the kingdoms of this world requires their citizens to offer their livelihoods for the maintenance of the king, and indeed their lives for his power, the opposite happens in Messiah's realm: he gives his life up for the sake of his people's lives, going a long step beyond even the Psalm-king's "precious is their blood in his sight", which commits the king to act for their lives, but not to give up his own.

In the final conflict of the Gospel of Mark two concepts of justice are in collision, with apparently fatal results to the bearer of one of them. But that one is the justice of God, and this is why it is ultimately victorious. Jesus leaves the tomb empty and goes before his disciples into Galilee, the scene of the establishment of his servant authority. Here, it is implied, that ministry will be begun over again through his disciples, to whom he gave authority over the unclean spirits; and they will preach the good news, the *euangelion* of the servant Messiah, throughout the world, and if necessary will drink the cup that he drank and be baptized with the baptism with which he was baptized, before he comes with the clouds of heaven to gather his elect.

Christian readers of Mark will naturally identify their time with the time of the preaching of the gospel throughout the world (13:10; 14:9), and perhaps themselves with the preachers. A careful and reflective reading of the Gospel will suggest how they may exercise that ministry in accord with the imperatives of messianic justice. They will act in accordance with human need, especially the needs of the poor, and not according to arbitrary rules. They will attempt to deliver all those under the power of Satan or under human oppression, no matter the religious or political necessity urged for such oppression. Like Jesus, they will often engage in symbolic action as a forecast of the full liberation yet to be achieved. Yet when they meet those who exploit others, their response will prefer forgiveness to condemnation and retribution, while never compromising on the inclusiveness of the messianic community. They will never forget that their Lord's blood was shed for *many*, without defining who the many are. They are simply those who need his forgiveness. They will be ready to take up their cross and follow him even to death; but they will be following one who is alive, who has gone before them into Galilee, and they will be alert for his coming, "at evening, at midnight, at cockcrow or at dawn" (13:35).

Chapter 7

THE STORY OF OUR WORLD

From time to time, as we have looked at conceptions of justice in the Bible, we have noticed connections, parallels or contrasts with life as we know it today. In this chapter we shall look in a sustained way at today's world and assess its achievement of justice with the help of what we have seen in the Bible. This is what I call a "justice audit". It takes the three narratives of justice that I have identified (in reverse order), and examines to what extent they can be told of our world. We shall need to keep in mind also the different levels on which we might expect to find justice being done: the personal, the local, the national and the global. As far as the first three are concerned, my focus will be on personal and local situations of which I am aware, and then mainly on my own country, the United Kingdom, and to some extent also, subject to the limitations of my knowledge, on the United States.

In looking at justice on the global level we need to grasp the fact that the world as we know it today is one world in a sense it has never been before, and certainly was not at the time of the Bible. The king of Assyria's exploitation did not affect the Chinese peasant. The economic machine of the Roman empire gained nothing from the farmers of West Africa. What we mean by globalization is that every part of the world is involved in a single economic system. Consumer goods are made in China, for example, in factories put up by, say, Dutch companies with money from banks in the City of London, which have been investing funds deposited with them by Saudi Arabian princes, who got rich by selling oil to the Americans, who are running a budget deficit financed by Chinese savings. The factories are staffed by poor migrants from the Chinese countryside, and their goods are sold in Britain (etc.) to people who are at the same time buying food grown in Kenya, or fed on fodder grown in Brazil, where peasants have been edged off the land and forests cleared by American multinationals using money gained from their dealings in ... But need I go on? The questions most sharply posed to us by our globalized system are: who has power, who benefits from it, and who has no power and loses from it? These are the questions of justice.

A Justice Audit of the Twenty-first-century World

A Community of Equals?

We have seen that the Old Testament, particularly the Torah, presupposes that Israel, the people addressed by the law, is a community of equal "brothers", a society consisting of families whose heads deal with each other on equal terms, and who have been given fair shares in the land that YHWH has given them; a people all of whose members are holy. Likewise in the New Testament fellow-Christians are brothers and sisters, and should be treated as such. We also saw defects in the way in which these ideas of equality were worked out in practice: there are unequals as well as equals in the Bible. All the same, the idea of a community of equals is worth comparing with the reality of societies in our day as well as in that of the Bible.

In today's world much noise is made in favour of democracy and freedom, but less is said about equality. This is wise, since in some ways the modern world is very unequal. However, there is more than one way in which we may measure equality, and thus more than one way in which we may believe that our own society fulfils the biblical ideal. We may assert that all human beings are equal in the sight of God. This is a purely theological or metaphysical assertion which requires no evidence and can be neither proved nor disproved. It does not distinguish an equal society from an unequal one.

Then there are social and political equality, and equality before the law, which often go together, though not always. There are certain societies with strongly held beliefs that everyone (originally, and often still, every *man*) is "as good as anyone else". In the United States it is a disadvantage for a political candidate to appear to be superior in education and intellect. This damaged John Kerry's campaign in 2004, while George W. Bush shrewdly presented himself as a man of the people, "just regular folks", gaining political advantage from this despite being the son of a former president and possessing great personal wealth. In the same country no one is legally debarred from civil rights by virtue of race, sex, class, or any other feature by which one person may be thought inferior to any other. At the other extreme as regards social (but not political) equality is India, where every person is born into a caste and can never escape from the social ranking which this determines: it is fixed for life. This is particularly oppressive for those who belong to no caste and are at the bottom of the hierarchy, those who used to be known as outcastes or untouchables; they themselves prefer the term *dalits*.

It is clear from the example of the United States that social equality and political equality are not everything. Although it is believed that all are created equal, only persons of substantial means can easily gain office in a political system where individuals are expected to compete for their party's nomination in primary elections. And the United States experiences greater economic inequality than any other developed country (except Singapore), with effects that we shall explore shortly (Wilkinson and Pickett 2009: 17). It is clear that belief in equality here functions as an ideology in the sense I defined in Chapter 1 (p. 4). The belief that people are equal in America, that anyone can succeed and even reach the top if they believe in themselves and work hard, blinds Americans to the extreme inequalities and injustices of their society. The great majority earn far less than their own bosses and may well have inadequate health insurance or education. There are also differences of race and gender in the distribution of wealth, income and social status. It may be that the advance in social and political equality for women and African Americans means that barriers to *individual* advancement are slowly coming down; the problem remains that there are huge inequalities between *classes* built into the system, *regardless* of race and gender.

The form of equality that has most impact on people's actual living conditions is economic equality. We have seen that the biblical community of equals does not imply strict material equality; but it does require a broad equality, or an equal sharing, of access to resources. Here I shall take equality in a broad sense, the equal distribution of wealth and income, and equal access to services such as education and health care. Sen emphasizes the distribution of "capabilities" as a measure of justice (Sen 2009: 253–90), pointing out that resources only matter for what one is able to do with them; and if you have a disability, for example, you need more resources to be capable of the same things as an able-bodied person (258–60); or if women are kept down in your society, having resources will be less use to you if you are a woman than if you are a man (257). Information collected on a global scale, which I detail below, mainly concerns income and wealth; but we should bear in mind in reading it that over much of the world gender, race and disability make inequality even more severe than simple inequality of income and wealth. The distribution of power is affected in all these ways. Power in most places is in the hands of wealthy men, usually able-bodied.

In global terms the world is extremely unequal. Milanovic (2002) shows that in 1993 the bottom 50% of the world population (households) received 8.5% of the household income in the world or spent 8.5% of the household expenditure, while the top 10% had just over 50%. (The article is based on a mixture of income surveys and expenditure surveys.) This is mainly due to differences between countries rather than within them, even though many countries are very unequal.

> The top 10 percent of the US population has an aggregate income equal to the income of the poorest 43 percent of people in the world, or differently put, total income of the richest 25 million Americans is equal to total income of almost 2 billion people. (Milanovic 2002: 50)

Since 1993 world inequality may have decreased owing to the rapid increase in incomes in China and India, but this increase itself has left most of Africa behind and has increased inequality *within* China and India (in China 0.1% of the population own 40% of the wealth, and 1% own 61% (Nolan 2009)). Thus there may be as many as a billion people with a bare minimum of food and shelter, while even middle-income people in the richer parts of the world take a variety of food, private cars, houses with private space for every member of the family, frequent air travel, etc., for granted – it has probably not yet sunk in that this level of luxury is unsustainable for large numbers of people.

The ownership of wealth is even more unequal than income. A study by the United Nations University World Institute for Development Economics Research, according to a press release (UNU-WIDER 2006), shows that the richest 2% of adults owned more than half of global assets in 2000, and the richest 1% owned 40%. The poorer 50% owned 1% of it. Further, wealthy individuals are largely concentrated in North America, Europe and wealthy countries in the East-Asia-Pacific area. Ownership of wealth does not affect living conditions as directly as income. Some apparently well-off individuals in rich countries actually have negative net wealth, because their debts (mainly mortgage debt) exceed their assets. But it is a sure guide to the distribution of power.

Tom Wolfe's sobriquet "the masters of the universe" for the people running the Wall Street banks has become an ironic cliché in the fallout from their recent difficulties (Wolfe 1988). This has perhaps obscured for us the reality that the phrase pointed to. The former and probably present power of the banks was not small. It was they who directed the flow of credit from the world's pension funds, insurance companies and other institutions with money to spare to industrial undertakings and governments, to farmers, and right down to people putting down money on a house or a car. It was they who determined the pattern of investment in the world economy, and governments, even the mighty US government, danced to their tune – indeed many members of US administrations have been and are bankers.

The modern world is not formally hierarchical. Power does not necessarily go with office or titles. Yet there is undoubtedly a hierarchy of power, trickling down from the bankers, directors of multinationals and the governments of rich countries, so often closely involved with them, to other states and ultimately, in vanishingly small amounts, to the peasants and workers of the world. In many countries, because of the modern world's concern for what is known as democracy, the humblest people are given a say from time to time on who should rule them. Rarely, however, is it possible for them to choose rulers who will not themselves be obedient to the dictates of more powerful governments, the multinationals operating in their territory and the banks. Thus political equality is largely illusory when economic equality does not exist.

What of economic equality within countries? This varies very greatly. Richard Wilkinson and Kate Pickett (2009) use for evidence 23 developed countries with a wide range of equality profiles, and also the 50 states of the USA. One simple way of comparing societies that they use asks by how many times the income of the richest fifth of the population, on average, exceeds that of the poorest fifth. The range among the 23 countries used extends from Japan, where this factor is 3.4, with the Nordic countries not far above, to the United States, where it is 8.5 (Wilkinson and Pickett 2009: 17). The United Kingdom, which became very much more unequal between 1979 and 1991, lies well towards the top end of the range at 7.2 (235). But even in the UK and the USA the majority of income is received by the middle classes. In most less developed countries the middle class is much smaller, and the spread of income is even wider, as the many poor people are poorer than the great majority in even the less affluent developed countries. Wealth, as in the world as a whole, is more unevenly spread within countries than income; in the UK between 2006 and 2008 9% of household wealth was owned by 50% of the households and 91% by the other 50%; the top 20% of households owned 62% of household wealth (ONS 2009: xxi).

The interest of Wilkinson and Pickett's book lies in its demonstration that most of the ills that afflict societies with advanced economies are more severe where inequality is greater, and that in such economies equality matters more than the total income per head. The USA, which has the highest income and the highest inequality, has the most mental illness, the largest proportion of its people in prison, the highest percentage of obese people, and the highest number of births per 1000 teenagers. The UK has less of each of these afflictions, but more than nearly all countries that are lower on the inequality scale. Japan is the most equal society in the world, and it scores lowest, or near to the bottom, on all of these measures of social stress. Other countries are strung out in between, with relatively few striking outliers. If all these measures are combined, all the countries turn out close to a straight line on the graph, with no outliers (20, 174). Most remarkably, levels of literacy and health (as measured by death rates) are lower in more unequal societies not only for the poor but also for the well-off (84, 180–87). The death rate for the top social class in England and Wales is higher than for the lowest social class in more equal Sweden. This may well be connected with the facts noted by Wilkinson and Pickett that more severe stress is created by threats to self-esteem or social status than by anything else (38, following Dickerson and Kemeny 2004), and that anxiety in individuals has increased with inequality (33–35, following Twenge 2007). The most basic difference arising from inequality is surely trust within society (49–62) and other consequences will flow from that.

It is of course obvious that a nation like Britain with its history of aristocratic rule, where social snobberies and jealousies, deference and resentment, jostle thickly, can in no way claim to be a society of equals. Its present economic inequalities reinforce the sense of mutual distance that is the heritage of its past social (and extreme economic) inequality. The shared experience of common struggle in total warfare against the common enemy between 1939 and 1945 brought our people together for a time, but the resumption of the race for affluence after the war drove us apart again. We are theoretically equal before the law and in our civil and political rights, but this is not enough to make us brothers and sisters, and even that legal equality is made less effective by our economic inequality.

It is more striking how divided the ideologically equal society of the United States is in reality. The republic was founded on the proposition that all were created equal, and in its early years understood that true liberty was impossible without equality. The leitmotif of de Tocqueville's great study of *Democracy in America*, based on a visit in 1831, is equality – its first sentence is "Of all the novel things that attracted my attention during my stay in the United States, none struck me more forcibly than the equality of social conditions" (de Tocqueville 2003: 11). But today the republic has become an engine for the creation of inequality. The change is connected with a change in the conception of liberty. For the founding fathers, as for Tom Paine, it meant freedom from domination, by kings for example. Today it tends to mean the freedom to do what one likes, especially to make money, without interference from the state, and without concern for the freedom of those from whom one makes it. (See further Sen 2009: 299–317.)

It is true that race has much to do with inequality in the USA, and not much less in the UK. At the time of the declaration of independence, the people held to be equal did not in practice include black slaves, and the inheritance of their treatment as second-class humans persists not only in the South, but everywhere, even with a black president. But the divide between rich and poor does not coincide with the racial divide. The capitalist system, left to itself, creates inequality regardless of race. The huge differences in opportunity and in access to services mean that however convinced people may be of their own equal value, the tenants of the condominiums of Manhattan and the slums of New Orleans cannot in practice live in the same world.

Justice as Faithfulness?

Given that the modern world is deeply unequal in most areas, we may nevertheless expect a commitment by those in positions of responsibility for others – parents, employers, government ministers, civil servants, social workers, teachers, doctors, hospital administrators – to the welfare of those for whom they are responsible. In modern industrial societies, at least in the West, we do not find patronage as a distinct feature separate from institutions and systems of employment and welfare, but in many parts of the world it is going strong (Eisenstadt and Roniger 1984). Commitment to others on a personal level could not be expected on a global scale; but as there is now a dense network of organizations and meetings co-operating internationally on matters of welfare and security – the United Nations, UNICEF, the World Trade Organization, the European Union, the World Health Organization, the G20 and many others, and billions of people receive help from them – it is legitimate to ask how far they truly serve their interests.

Clearly this is a question which requires a separate answer for every individual or institution of which it is asked, and an attempt to give a general answer would not give useful information. But it is possible to chart certain trends.

As industrial society developed in Great Britain, the relationships surviving from feudal society, such as the patronage in rural society of villagers by the landowner, withered and died. Frequently, patronage relationships were invaded by commercial considerations and tenants, who had always been at the landlord's mercy, became simply cash cows. Thus in England in the eighteenth century common land, where villagers had been accustomed to collect firewood and graze their animals, was enclosed in most places for the exclusive use of landowners. In the highlands of Scotland between 1745 and 1850, clan chiefs became mere lairds, effectively repudiating their responsibility for their clanspeople, whom many of them drove off their land to enable them to pasture sheep on it (the "clearances"). In the growing industrial towns, labour was generally treated as a mere factor of production, paid at the lowest rate that would keep body and soul together. Most employers took no responsibility for the welfare of their workers; housing was provided by speculative builders, and medical care hardly existed; education was a voluntary service largely provided, if at all, by the Church. But there was a significant minority of industrialists who had a care for their workers, building housing for them and providing some essential services, such as education for their apprentices.

In the course of the nineteenth and twentieth centuries there were two significant developments. One was that key welfare services such as education and health, and to some extent housing, which had previously been provided on a voluntary or commercial basis, were largely taken over by the state. The other was that employers were more and more expected or required to ensure the health and safety of their workers as long as they were at work, and to pay wages that would do more than simply keep someone alive. Their minimum level tended to increase, and a minimum wage was legislated for all workers from 1998. The hours of work required steadily decreased up to the mid-twentieth century. As Sen argues is invariably true (Sen 2009: 338–54), the advance of democracy and liberal institutions such as a free press and free trade unions, enabling citizens to hold government and employers to account – what Sen describes as "government by discussion" – were very important factors in these achievements. But Sen also points out (351) that the mere existence of the institutions is not enough; they need active citizens to enable them to do their job. Thus, even though such institutions scarcely existed in the biblical world, the need is still the same: people who care for their neighbours and for the health of their society.

In this country there has been a long history of public provision for the destitute, or those likely to become so: those who were unable to work, or unable to find work. But this has never been without conditions, most notoriously in the Poor Law of 1834, which demanded supervised work in the workhouse as the price of maintenance. One effect of this public provision, not always remarked on, is to create the assumption that it is entirely the responsibility of government (local or national) to ensure that its people should not be destitute – and therefore that individuals have no such responsibility, other than through their taxes. On the first page of Charles Dickens's first published book, before the passing of the 1834 Poor Law, we read: "What can [the poor man] do? To whom is he is he to apply for relief? To private charity? To benevolent individuals? Certainly not – there is his parish" (Dickens n.d.: 1). There is a clear contrast with Muslim countries, where *zakat*, generally understood as the giving of alms to the poor, is one of the basic responsibilities of all men, one of the five pillars of Islam. There is another contrast with African (and other) societies, where there is a responsibility to support even relatively remote members of one's own family. Most of these countries have no substantial system of state-provided welfare. They could not afford it in any case, but it is possible that it is not seen as necessary to the same extent because of the widespread sense of personal obligation.

Thus, although most people give something to charity in this country, the biggest sums are collected for medical and animal charities, and few exercise any personal responsibility for the livelihoods of the poor in this country. Moreover, communities have lost cohesiveness – this is another effect of affluence combined with inequality – so that most people would not be aware of those needing help in their local area. In fact, communities are not only less cohesive, they are also more segregated on class lines, so that middle class people even in a relatively small city such as Oxford are barely aware of the existence and needs of poor and working-class people living in council estates a few miles from their doors, where most people have enough to do to keep themselves in decent order, and have little to spare for their neighbours.

But there is also a heritage from the ideology of the 1834 Poor Law; most people believe that giving money to beggars discourages self-reliance, and many extend this even to the receipt of state benefits; present government policy seems to concur, requiring recipients of disability benefit and single mothers of young children to prepare themselves for work. Needless to say, beliefs of this kind are also widespread, and even more influential, in the USA.

We seem to have the worst of both worlds. There is no encouragement for people to develop a serious sense of direct personal responsibility towards poorer fellow-citizens as there is in Muslim or family-orientated societies, while at the same time, as most or all of most people's taxes is deducted at source, taxation does not involve them in taking active steps to fulfil their responsibility. Quite the reverse: all the activity among citizens in regard to taxation is devoted to avoiding it. There is no serious advocacy of the payment of taxes as a social good. Shifting our attention to corporations, many of the biggest devote resources to ever more complex artificial ways of avoiding taxation, and justify this by pointing to their fiduciary responsibility to their shareholders to maximize returns. This is significant, for while they have a legal responsibility to pay taxes that they have legally incurred, they have no similar fiduciary responsibility to society as a whole to shoulder their share of society's burden. To put it another way, company law places certain legal obligations on companies, but defines the purpose of their existence as being to make profits for their shareholders, without any broader purpose. Will Hutton's consideration of "capitalisms" (1995: 257–84), suggests some different possibilities. Can we define our society as just if the institutions that dominate our economy are thus effectively prevented (with their own eager acquiescence!) from contributing to the full to its justice? We shall return to this question shortly.

Personal responsibility has perhaps been better organized to support global justice than internal justice, but of course this only makes up for a far greater shortfall in public provision (see below). In the UK, as in other countries, there exist large charities which raise money here and work with partners in the less developed world for famine and disaster relief in the first place, but more importantly for development, and also work in this country for development education and campaigning for global justice. These are often of Christian inspiration – Christian Aid, Tearfund and others. By the standards of charities these raise very large sums, but they are generally in the tens, rarely hundreds, of millions of pounds. Christian Aid, for example, raised £86.5 million in 2007–08, of which £66 million went directly to its charitable activities (Charity Commission 2009). The largest development charity in the UK, Oxfam, had an income of nearly £300m in approximately the same year. Some of their supporters may give sacrificially, and many to serious effect, but the average amount put in the envelope in Christian Aid Week is less than a pound. They affect for the better the lives of thousands or even millions of people in the developing world, but in comparison with their total numbers these are few.

Again, in the absence of fair trade agreed at the level of governments, a citizens' fair trade movement has emerged, which has even engaged some of the big retailers and manufacturers in the UK – all Sainsbury's bananas are fairly traded, and Cadbury's Dairy Milk chocolate is now made only from fairly traded cocoa. The fair-trade mark is affixed to products which are bought directly from the producers, or their co-operatives, at a price which gives a fair return to the individual producers and includes a premium to enable the development of their communities. The same thing can be said of these excellent ventures as of the development charities: they have transformed the lives of many, but billions more remain untouched.

The sad conclusion must be that despite the honest commitment of many, justice as faithfulness between the developed and the developing world remains a distant dream.

Finally in this section something must be said of justice in the courts, since we mentioned it in Chapter 4 as having a relationship to Paul's conception of justification. I said there: Suppose that in reality and not merely in theory the object of justice were to reconcile the criminal with the community? The policies pursued at present by the legislature and the courts, in all the countries of the UK and in most of the states of the USA, has led to longer and longer prison sentences and prisons too full to be able to fulfil their supposed function of rehabilitating the prisoner. In the UK this has happened while crime rates have actually been falling. Interesting experiments have been undertaken in so-called "restorative justice", which brings the offender face to face with the victim; and so-called "community sentences" have become quite widely used for lesser offences: these require the offender to undertake unpaid work for the community for a certain number of hours. Yet this is tinkering at the margins. Prison achieves little for most offenders. In the USA, 40% to 50% of prisoners released in 1994 had been convicted once again after three years (US Department of Justice 2002). Our criminal justice systems are not reconciling the offender with the community, and perhaps have never been intended to.

Justice as Right Order?

In relation to the narrative of justice we examined in Chapter 3, the question for our audit is how, if at all, the order of divine justice is shown in the ruling systems and orders of our world. Here, in view of the cosmic setting of the underlying concept, we should look at how justice is or is not being done by human beings to the natural world, as well as in human society. In view of our earlier analyses, we should ask not just what states are doing, but about the effects of the global economic system which has most states in its thrall.

Since the autumn of 2008 this system has been in crisis. Banks have collapsed or been rescued with large amounts of government money. The continuous growth which is presented as the *raison d'être* of the system has gone into reverse. The UK economy contracted by about 6% in the 18 months to the end of September 2009 (Guardian 2009). But this should not encourage one to think that radical change is on the way. It is characteristic of markets to fall as well as to rise. This is the greatest fall since the 1930s, but there is nothing to suggest that the rising curve will not be resumed in due course, as stock markets have already done in anticipation. Governments are doing their best to ensure that financial institutions are stabilized and that we return to business as usual as soon as possible.

But we need to examine with a sceptical eye what "business as usual" in the global marketplace actually means. A market economy is one in which not only goods and services are sold, but also all that is required to provide them: raw materials, labour, and capital. All who are involved buy at the cheapest price they can obtain and sell at the dearest. Classical economic theory asserts that in this way everyone gets the best bargain; this is a form of justice, in which everyone is paid the proper cost of what they provide. But this theory ignores the disparity in power between different players in the market; and when dealing in a global marketplace power differentials can be extreme. It is a serious weakness of Sen's book that he does not discuss inequality of power as a threat to justice. Those with great power get the best bargains; those with little or no power get poor ones. This is injustice.

The Costs of Growth

Business as usual means that growth should be resumed as soon as possible. It is fundamental to the ideology of the global market system that economic growth is a good thing, and that so far as possible it should continue indefinitely. The necessity of growth to market capitalism, its unsustainability, and alternatives to it are discussed in penetrating detail by Tim Jackson (2009). For peoples at a low point of development growth *is* good: it gives them benefits in health, education and security, as well as useful goods (Sen 2009: 347). But beyond a certain point the real benefits of growth begin to tail off, as was pointed out by J. K. Galbraith more than fifty years ago (Galbraith 1958). People do not get any happier as their economies grow beyond a certain point; indeed the nations with the happiest people include ones at all stages of development – Tanzania and Indonesia as well as Mexico and the USA (Wilkinson and Pickett 2009: 5–10, referring to Layard 2005). Sen's point is well taken that happiness is not necessarily a good criterion, since people adapt to the deprivation they experience, if they do not expect it to improve (Sen 2009: 282–83). But Wilkinson and

Pickett show the same thing even more clearly for life expectancy, a much more objective criterion (2009: 6–7). While averages are considerably lower for the poorest countries, they are already above 70 for nations as poor as Egypt, Nicaragua and Serbia, and are as high in Cuba and Costa Rica as in the USA.

Why then is growth insisted on as an absolute good? It is ostensibly urged because it creates jobs, and because it provides the wealth from which taxes can be paid for the improvement of services which benefit the community. But these are pretexts: growth does not deliver more jobs once there is full employment (cf. Galbraith 1958: 150); and if public spending is thought to be a good thing it can and should take a greater share of the available wealth. In fact growth is the natural effect, during good times, of a competitive market economy. Enterprises compete with one another for a share of the market, and so encourage their customers to buy more. If there are relatively easy financial conditions, all will see a growth in their business: the total size of the market will have increased. The opposite happens when credit is scarce, as now. The shareholders of companies expect them to produce profits, and these are greater if the economy is booming. Further, as Tim Jackson shows (2009: 62–65), in such an economy there is always a drive for greater labour productivity, which must increase either output or unemployment. Growth is therefore necessary to the smooth working of such an economy; so its urging as an absolute good is ideological in the sense I defined in Chapter 1.

But growth does not come without cost. The inequality which we studied earlier in this chapter is one effect of uncontrolled growth. Growth may result in higher incomes for all, but much more so for the owners and managers of businesses than for their workers, since the former will attempt to limit wage increases, and much less so for those without work. Another effect is the kind of speculative bubble created by easy credit which affected the property market over the 15 years up to 2007, and ended in the inevitable crash, causing loss and misery to thousands. A third is the destruction of traditional communities and social connectedness by the churning effect, geographical and cultural, of constant innovation.

All these are types of injustice and disorder. They can be moderated by government control and guidance, as for example the control of inequality by redistribution in the Nordic countries, or by cultural restraints, as with the equalization of rewards in Japan (Wilkinson and Pickett 2009: 176). But the fourth effect is much more difficult to moderate, and that is the effect on the environment.

This essential actor in the market has no power at all, at least not at the point of the transaction. The earth is the ultimate source of all raw materials and the ultimate destination of all the waste that the system produces, from carbon dioxide to plastic bags. Since it has no power it is unable to levy a charge for its services. If it was able to do so, and did so at their true cost, most of the activities of the system would be priced out of existence. Thus we discover that the global economic system impoverishes natural systems in order to enrich (some) human beings. This process is described as the creation of wealth; but how much wealth is created rather than merely transferred can only be measured properly if the earth's losses are set against human beings' gains. In any case, if there is no compensation, if forests are not replanted (together, impossibly, with all the variety of species that they sheltered), if fish stocks are not replenished, land degraded by intensive agriculture not restored, species destroyed by global warming not (impossibly again) replaced, the just rule of God in creation, the order which is celebrated by heaven and earth and sea, by field and trees (Ps. 96.11–12, cf. 98.7–8), is set at nought. This is injustice. (For a full treatment from a biblical point of view see the volume in this series by David Horrell (Horrell 2010), or Bauckham 2010.)

Moreover, the wealth supposedly created is now seen to be only temporary; as wastes accumulate the earth becomes less habitable, and the costs simply of maintaining the human presence climb to insupportable levels. Thus the system impoverishes future generations in order to enrich the present. This also is injustice.

Exploitation

The market economy's fundamental dynamic of buying cheap includes, of course, the hire of labour, and in a global economy the producers of goods (and even some services, such as call centres) have increasingly chosen to locate their factories wherever local wages are lowest, as long as the required skills are available. Though this will be seen as an injustice by the workers in more affluent countries who have lost their jobs, it is unlikely to be seen in that way by people who have got the new jobs. But unless they are enlightened by a trade union or some other agency, they may not be aware of how much the goods they make sell for, and so not realize the size of the profits they are making for their masters.

The relationship between the employing and employed classes in the capitalist system is defined in the Marxist tradition as one of exploitation, that is, that part of the proper reward of the labour of the workers is appropriated by the capitalists. This is not of course an undisputed concept.

For Marx it arose because he espoused the "labour theory of value", according to which the value of goods is equal to the total labour embodied in them (including the labour which went to create the capital employed; see, e.g., Marx 1959: 147). Profit taken by the capitalist class then represents part of the value created by labour. Many economists would dispute the analysis, without denying that exploitation occurs. But, without entering on a detailed economic argument, it is possible to note the direction in which the proportion of turnover devoted to wages and other objects moves, and if one finds wages have declined on average in relation to dividends and the rewards of the directors, it is reasonable to speak of exploitative tendencies in the labour market.

And this has been true over the last 30 or so years, especially starkly so in the USA, where average real wages remained approximately constant between 1974 and 2007, while the wealth of the country expanded enormously (Wasow *et al.* 2008). Labour was not being given an equitable share in the rising rewards of business. Household income only rose because people worked longer. The purely monetary side of it is not all. Over the same 30 years, in the USA and the UK, security of employment has tended to decline, and the pressure to fulfil rising expectations has increased. Work has become less satisfying, more pressured, and more insecure. In these circumstances capitalism has demonstrated its tendency to enrich owners (shareholders) at the expense of wage-workers. This too is injustice.

Buying cheap also applies to raw materials. The power of multinational companies is exercised to extract minerals in poor countries with low rewards to workers often working in dangerous or unhealthy conditions, and with devastating effects on the environment. The same applies to agricultural products. These may be produced in plantations with the same consequences, and in addition very often that of destroying pristine environments such as tropical rain forest. In Brazil the Amazon forest continues to be felled to create ranches or to grow soya. Thus, still, as in colonial times, the economic system tends to enrich the "centre", that is, the developed lands where the enterprises are based, at the expense of the periphery. This is why many writers speak of "neo-colonialism". This too is injustice.

Justice and the State
We have explored the numerous ways in which the market economy tends to enrich the powerful at the expense of the weak: the human species at the expense of all others, the present generation at the expense of future generations, owners at the expense of those who can only contribute their

labour, and the centre at the expense of the periphery. This is how the system operates untrammelled. But it is possible to control it and moderate its effects, as we have already noted. The institution which is best placed to do this is the state, and we have seen that in biblical thought the protection of the poor from oppression is one of the principal functions of the state, in the figure of the king. We need to ask how well modern states are fulfilling this task.

It must be said straight away that the great majority of states are puny by comparison with the might of the capitalist system as a whole, especially when that is backed up as it often is by the pressure of the most powerful states and international organizations such as the IMF. The whole economy of many countries is smaller than that of many multinational companies that operate within them, and the state in the least developed countries is always weak; it does not have the resources to raise large amounts of taxes, to prevent corruption or to control economic activity. Our attention needs to be given to the governments of the richer countries, which are in a position to do all these things. They are capable of regulating capitalism as it operates in their territories, and also of affecting the operations of corporations based in their territories in the rest of the world, especially by joint action through international organizations.

All these states do in fact give oversight to the operation of the market in their countries, and there are many aspects in which this oversight operates in similar ways in them all. Fraud and corruption is detected and punished, contracts are enforced by the courts, and in other ways the market is helped to work efficiently and honestly. None of this, of course, serves to protect the poor, except from dishonest dealing, which affects everyone. More significantly, all developed countries have laws to limit hours worked, to enforce the timely payment of wages, and to ensure safety at work, and many have a legal minimum wage. All have some form of social insurance, which enables workers to receive benefits when unemployed or off sick, and an old age pension. All also have provision to maintain those without insurance, or who have exhausted it, at a minimum level. But they differ in the extent to which the activities of trade unions (labour unions) are protected, and where, as in the USA, unions are weak and relatively unprotected, it is relatively easy for employers to put pressure on workers to accept worse conditions of work and to sack them at short notice. In other countries, such as Germany and Japan, this is much more difficult.

Some aspects of life are not left to the market in most of these countries. All of them have systems of state education, which educate the great majority of children. Most of them (the USA is the big exception) have universal systems of health insurance, usually with publicly administered hospitals. In many of them (more until 30 years ago) there are state-owned railways, communications and energy supplies.

There is a far greater degree of justice for the poor in developed countries now than there was in the past, or for that matter in most less developed countries – for experience shows that to rely on individual generosity or on family help is to rely on what is unpredictable, highly variable and arbitrary in principle. Welfare benefits in Britain today may not be generous, but they are secure and predictable, and they are backed up by the public services I have mentioned. There are serious questions about their adequacy, especially as they leave the poor in the position of being unable to share in life in the same way as others in the community. While being uprated in line with inflation, they have failed to keep pace with wages and therefore with the general standard of living in British society, making a significant contribution to the rising inequality explored in the last section. But at least they give a living. The most shocking domestic measures passed by British parliaments of recent times are the withdrawal of all benefits from 16- and 17-year-olds under the Thatcher government, and the similar withdrawal of benefits from rejected claimants for asylum under the recent Labour government. These measures have broken the tacit contract that the state will not leave people destitute. In the case of asylum seekers this is not mere meanness; the object is to compel them to leave the country, and the measure is of a piece with the general inhumane treatment of their persons and the frequent refusal, for no good reason, to believe their stories.

In perhaps 50 countries of the modern world, the state is in broad terms fulfilling its brief to protect the poor within its borders, but with many exceptions and failures, whether deliberate or negligent. It is doing so more effectively than any ancient Israelite government ever did, hobbled as they were by the contradiction that in ancient Israel and Judah the main engine of exploitation was the state itself. And it does so because in these countries there is "government by discussion", and the related culture and institutions (Sen 2009: 321–54; see 111).

It is when we come to *global* action for justice that we discover the most profound failure of the modern state. We find that the most powerful states, France, the UK, and above all the USA devote much of their diplomatic and military efforts to protecting their economic interests around the world. This has generally meant promoting trade in their own manufactures and exerting pressure on foreign governments to dismantle any barriers such as tariffs intended to protect their own competing products, while maintaining their own barriers to agricultural products from the developing world. The ruling elite of the developing country may be bribed or flattered or intimidated into agreeing, and ignore the interests of the poor masses whom they theoretically represent. The liberalization in favour of the developed countries is thus added to the inherent imbalance of power in trade between rich and poor which makes nonsense of the neo-liberal belief that free markets will always produce results advantageous to both parties. Forty to sixty years after the end of political colonialism, most former colonies remain underdeveloped with vast numbers of extremely poor people, farmers and increasingly also, with the increase in populations, unemployed or casually employed city dwellers. Truly fair trade would certainly have made some difference, although it is right to add that local governments and wealthy people must bear some of the responsibility for the state of their poor, especially in a country like India with its affluent and expanding middle class.

What is more shocking is that so frequently the economic interests of states are interpreted as freedom for the business undertakings of their citizens to exploit the resources and labour of poorer countries with little compensation, and that sometimes this is taken to justify interfering in the politics of foreign countries. Freely elected governments have been overthrown, ostensibly in order to protect countries from communism, in reality to protect expatriate enterprises. The most notorious examples are Iran in 1953, when Mohammed Mosaddeq had nationalized the Anglo-Iranian Oil Company and was removed by the Shah – an action inspired by the CIA and MI6 whose effects on relations between Iran and the West endure to this day; Guatemala in 1954, where the government of Jacobo Arbenz was removed by an operation inspired and funded by the CIA, largely at the instigation of the United Fruit Company; and Chile in 1973, when the coup led by General Pinochet overthrew the elected president, Salvador Allende, after months of disorder, much of it funded by the CIA. Strategic rather than economic considerations may have been uppermost here, but there is no question about the involvement of the American copper-mining companies and ITT in the opposition to Allende.

This dismal history has to be set against the programmes of foreign aid which the same countries promote. In any case, the element of self-interest in these programmes is plain. They are often conditional on making orders from companies based in the aid-giving country. The order of priorities is based on the aid-giving country's strategic interests: much of the aid is military, and the country receiving the greatest amount of US aid is Israel, which is small and by no means poor. In any case, the aid is far from generous. The United Nations has set a benchmark of 0.7% of GDP for its members to contribute through aid to the development needs of the poorer countries. Few of them have actually reached that mark, though it has existed for many years.

More recently, in 2000, the Millennium Development Goals were set by the UN General Assembly. Here the members undertook:

- To halve, by the year 2015, the proportion of the world's people whose income is less than one dollar a day and the proportion of people who suffer from hunger and, by the same date, to halve the proportion of people who are unable to reach or to afford safe drinking water.
- To ensure that, by the same date, children everywhere, boys and girls alike, will be able to complete a full course of primary schooling and that girls and boys will have equal access to all levels of education.
- By the same date, to have reduced maternal mortality by three-quarters, and under-five child mortality by two-thirds, of their current rates.
- To have, by then, halted, and begun to reverse, the spread of HIV/AIDS, the scourge of malaria and other major diseases that afflict humanity.
- To provide special assistance to children orphaned by HIV/AIDS.
- By 2020, to have achieved a significant improvement in the lives of at least 100 million slum dwellers as proposed in the "Cities Without Slums" initiative. (UN General Assembly Resolution 55/2, September 2000)

More than halfway to 2015, it cannot be said that the world is anything like halfway to these goals. The richer UN members have simply not stumped up the resources required. Justice is not a matter of fine words but of deeds.

Besides the United Nations, most of the states of the world are members of other international institutions intended to engage them in co-operative endeavours to open up trade, develop their economies, and secure them against financial disaster: the World Trade Organization, the World Bank and the International Monetary Fund, in addition to specialist agencies such as the World Health Organization. Most of the time, however, these agencies have worked against the interests of the poorest people in the less developed parts of the world.

The systemic failings of the IMF and the World Bank have been amply documented, for example by Joseph Stiglitz, a former Chief Economist of the World Bank (Stiglitz 2002). They are not controlled in equal shares by their membership: votes in the IMF are in proportion to the states' respective contributions, like a joint-stock bank, which means that it is controlled by the richer countries, largely by the USA. From the 1980s, it imposed "structural adjustment programmes" on states borrowing from it, often in desperate circumstances. These programmes were based on what Stiglitz calls "market fundamentalism", and involved deep cuts in budgets, cutting of food subsidies, liberalization of trade, and privatization of services such as water supply. The governments have had no choice but to accept these conditions, and if the IMF refuses to lend, so will other lenders (Stiglitz 2002: 27). But they almost always led to a contraction in the economy, and deepened the insecurity and poverty of the mass of the population. "IMF economists could ignore the short-term effects their policies might have on the country, content in the belief that *in the long run* the country would be better off; any adverse short-run impacts would be merely pain that was necessary as part of the process" (Stiglitz 2002: 36). No doubt Stiglitz is correct in implying that the IMF economists believed their own ideology, the so-called "Washington consensus". But the fact is that while these measures rarely served the interests of farmers and workers in the developing world, they were unquestionably profitable for bankers in the rich world. The WTO is certainly more democratic than the IMF, which is why it has had limited success in securing trade agreements: they must be agreed unanimously. Therefore the WTO is bypassed to enable bilateral agreements which are easier to secure.

Thus our audit of global justice ends with the sad conclusion that there is not much of it. The imbalances in resources and power make it virtually impossible for the weaker parties to contend for it effectively, and as ever the stronger have no interest in granting it of their own accord, and rarely any desire to do so.

Finally, do modern states protect cosmic justice? Are they active in protecting the natural environment against the effects of the market economy, or in protecting future generations against the depredations of the present generation? Yes, to some extent, but not enough, one has to say. Since the 1970s there has been awareness of the environmental damage of most economic activity, and governments have appointed ministers for the environment, and commissioned studies. Much progress has been made in reducing pollution, cleaning up rivers, stopping acid rainfall, saving forests, protecting wildlife, recycling waste, developing renewable energy sources.

But far too little has been done to combat global warming. The difficulty is evident. All the other problems are created by some part of the economy; but virtually *all* activity in the modern economy produces CO_2. To reduce emissions radically requires either a *planned* reduction in economic activity – and how contrary that is to the nature of a market economy we have already explored – or a total transformation in its power sources; and very likely both processes must be pursued at the same time in order to produce the necessary effect fast enough. There has indeed been action at the international level, with the Kyoto process, and its successor which was intended to come to final decisions at Copenhagen in December 2009, as I write. I do not know what conclusions this process will have come to by the time anyone reads these words. The signs are mixed. President Obama, for example, has pledged that the USA will cut its global warming emissions by 17% by 2020. This is simply not enough, when all the scientific evidence points to a need for very deep cuts *on 1990 levels* by 2030 (Monbiot 2006: 16). The earlier cuts are made, the greater the effect will be.

Must we then anticipate a catastrophic shattering of the just order of creation as we have experienced it over the whole of humanity's history up to now? All one can say is that that is the direction in which we are heading. To avoid this outcome requires what the Bible knows as repentance.

Chapter 8

OUR STORY: DOING JUSTICE IN OUR WORLD

We have looked at biblical narratives of God's justice and at the way in which biblical writers see them as being imitated or ignored in human action in the Bible's world. We have also looked at the extent to which they are embodied in our world today. Together these facts constitute the Bible's challenge to do justice. It is a challenge to the Church as embodied both in individual Christians and in the churches. I would argue, moreover, that it is not only a challenge for Christians or the Church. Obviously the narratives and laws of justice in the Hebrew Bible demand action from Jews. But a reader of the Bible does not have to be a believer of any sort to perceive challenges in its text; all that is necessary is, to use my words in Chapter 1 (p. 14), "the response of the imagination to the moral feeling evoked by the text, which is called forth in the same way by our own context".

Here we need to deal successively with the three biblical narratives of justice (in the order of this book) and ask how we could help them to be realized in our world – not just how they might in theory be realized, but specifically how individuals and churches acting either alone or, better, together as movements might make a difference. But not only this. We must also ask how Christians may and must follow the example of Jesus' practice of justice.

Justice as Right Order

The comprehensive character of the *wrong* order in which the modern world is organized, particularly as a global economic system, is only too likely to drive the average person, believer or non-believer, to desperation. Just what can one or a few people do to make any difference to this huge economic machine and its immensely wealthy drivers? The believer here does or should have the advantage precisely of belief: that God is in ultimate charge of the world, and will "judge the world with righteousness, and the peoples with his truth". For Christians, the hope of resurrection lies just beyond the seeming dereliction of Calvary. Historically, faith in God's ultimate victory has not led to quietism, but encouraged action by believers in support of the campaign. However, at this time there is little sign of especially vigorous activism on the part of Christians, except in certain fields – fair trade would be an example, or, from a different part of the Church theologically, the "right to life". But there are many things that can be done for a just world and just societies, even if they do not obviously promise immediate change.

There are some temptations to avoid: first, of course, the temptation of despair, with its sequel apathy, spiritually to be understood as *accidie* ("sloth"). But utopianism or unrealism is an equally dangerous one: that is the illusion that, so far from nothing being possible, everything can and will be done; it is likely in its turn to become apathy or conservatism when it becomes clear that the hoped-for revolution is not going to happen – witness those former Communists who populate the comment pages of right-wing newspapers. But in avoiding unrealism, we may fall into the opposite error of becoming unnecessarily complicit in the world's unjust systems. I say "unnecessarily", since the world economic system is all-embracing, and there is no way of avoiding some complicity. What is needed is realistic resistance to the system's demands in selected and well-defined situations, which must also be well-advertised, articulate and irenic so that it attracts as many supporters as possible.

This may take effect at a number of different levels. The most obvious one is that of the national political system wherever one resides. This idea is bound to arouse the objection that engagement in party politics itself entails unnecessary complicity in corruption and injustice. There is of course a view among Christians of a conservative persuasion that politics is "a dirty business" that should be avoided, and a variation that holds that while individuals have a right to be involved, the church as such should not express political opinions. But I do not expect that anyone who has read thus far in this book will share such views. The point is rather that the parliamentary system, or the constitutional system of the USA, is set up in such a way that rather than confronting or controlling the oppressions of the economic system it can only encourage or be complicit with them. It can hardly be denied that in the UK today disillusion with politics has reached unprecedented depths, and not without justification. There is no substantial difference in fundamental philosophy between the three main political parties: all have accepted the neo-liberal revolution of the 1980s, and points of dispute are at the margins. This means, let us be clear, that all three parties support a system which over the past 30 years has encouraged consumer luxury spending fuelled by credit, and deepened inequality and class segregation. As a result politics have become increasingly focused on personalities, with the consequent unpleasant personal attacks, while the people themselves have chosen largely to leave politics to the politicians, even as they dismiss the politicians as corrupt and self-seeking. Membership in political parties has dropped to historically low levels. In healthy political societies most of the enfranchised citizens take part in politics in one way or another. This was true of Britain in the nineteenth century, and as late as 1945 the Labour party was a mass party with more than a million members and general support from the working class.

But what is the conclusion? To avoid politics altogether means exacerbating the situation, or doing nothing to mend it, leaving the conduct of the nation's business to the present crowd of career politicians – or quite possibly to the racist nationalists who may succeed where they inevitably fail in exciting popular interest and support. However slight the support for constitutional politics, this is how things get done. If they are not done well by those we approve of, they will be done evilly by others. A more constructive alternative would be to join one or other of the main parties in order to turn them back to their original purposes, or to join and work for a party which has policies that accord better with the view of justice held out in this book: the Green party is the obvious choice. Neither approach may have any immediate prospect of success, though the Greens' successes in local elections and those based on proportional representation, as for the European parliament, should not be overlooked. But one or other choice is necessary, and in due course may bear fruit.

But this cannot be enough. Even where there is a representative political system, it is necessary for citizens to take action outside it to achieve change and spur the elected representatives into effective action. Action of this kind is best taken in common with others. There is a huge body of activist groups in this country dedicated to every conceivable cause. Where their cause is just and in no disagreement with Christian (or Jewish) faith, there is every reason why Christians or Jews should give them their support. A distinction needs to made between campaigning and direct action on the one hand, and charitable activities on the other, which are often carried out by the same associations: the latter belong to the next section, concerning justice as faithfulness. Among campaigning groups, to take a few examples, one might expect to find persons of faith supporting the campaigning activities of Christian Aid (but not specifically because of its Christian inspiration and direction); the Child Poverty Action Group; Greenpeace, with its manifold worldwide activities on behalf of the environment; the Campaign for Nuclear Disarmament; some of the anti-capitalist groups now springing up.

Many Christians feel queasy about direct action, which some but not most groups campaigning for justice engage in, perhaps because of the feeling that this is unlawful and may lead to violence, or indeed actually consists in violence. Some with such views have no problem with violence in other situations, particularly when authorized by duly constituted authority, such as war or judicial punishment; which suggests that the real problem is illegality rather than violence. It is worth pointing out that Jesus' so-called "cleansing of the Temple" was both unlawful and (moderately) violent (and, be it noted, makes Jesus' arrest and condemnation totally explicable and lawful in human terms). Is the disciple to be forbidden what the master allowed himself? Bonhoeffer and other Christians in the German resistance movement came to the conclusion that even assassination was permissible in the cause of resisting Nazism. The ethical question about this cannot be addressed here. But this is a very rare situation, for a single direct action cannot normally succeed in actually preventing an evil; it is primarily symbolic.

It is also possible and right for individuals to contribute directly in their everyday lives to the righting of the unjust relations between nations and between human beings and the natural world. We can all buy fair-trade goods, conserve energy in our homes, buy electricity which has been renewably generated as far as possible, abandon car use as far as possible, reduce or eliminate our eating of meat, and so forth.

Should campaigning action, in words or in deeds, be left to individuals, or should churches as bodies engage in it? The first thing to be said that is that it is not possible for a church to engage convincingly in action for a just world if justice does not reign within it. The witness of those churches in which ordination, or certain orders such as the episcopate, are barred to women, is seriously damaged as a result. The struggle for women's ordination is obviously a struggle for justice against a bad tradition, whatever the spurious theological arguments alleged in its favour; Christian feminists have always seen it as one with the campaign for enfranchisement and an effective women's voice in the secular world. This is not the only matter of justice to be settled within the Christian community, but it is one of the most obvious.

As there is a tradition of church conferences and assemblies passing resolutions on public matters, the question of church action has been decided in principle long since. However, resolutions generally achieve little; the real question confronting a church is whether it should engage in a persistent campaign against an injustice, for example against the inhuman way in which asylum seekers are treated in the UK, including mass writing of letters to MPs, marches and demonstrations and lobbying. A few years ago the churches very widely supported the Jubilee 2000 campaign for the remission of the debts of heavily indebted poor countries, and their support contributed much to the (modified) success of that campaign. It is clear that churches can be effective campaigning bodies, but only if they have general support from their membership, as this one did. One would not expect a campaign for a more progressive income tax, for example, to have the same support. A claim for asylum gains general support in the case of individuals who are known to the church members and plainly have a just cause; it is less certain that a general campaign would garner equally wide support. But it is important that individuals should not be deterred from activity by lack of support from their churches.

Justice as Faithfulness

It ought to go without saying that a person who argues for justice should practise justice. In the first place, this means being faithful to personal obligations. Traditionally, the just pay their debts, keep their promises, including their marriage vows, respect their superiors, look after their parents in their old age, treat their children with affection and gentle firmness, and are fair to those they employ or manage.

It is not to be taken for granted that persons of faith do all these things, but supposing that they do, the Bible has further challenges for them. Those taught by Scripture are not just fair to those in their employ (this is required by law in advanced countries in any case), but gentle and generous, and mindful of their personal needs: for example they will pay above the minimum wage, and make every effort to meet requests for flexible working hours and extra maternity leave beyond the statutory requirement. The same goes for other situations where one person has power over others: for teachers in schools, judges in court, or police in the streets, not least in those tense situations created by public protest (generally for justice, however interpreted!) or the threat of terrorism. It is precisely in those situations where just conduct is most difficult because of the emotions aroused by them that it is most necessary, and most praiseworthy, to keep calm and do what is just.

The just make an effort to accommodate those with disabilities and problems. They give generously to those in need, sometimes directly, but in modern conditions more often through organized charities that channel help to the needy at home or abroad; the better of those charities working abroad take as their prime goal the development of poor communities to become self-reliant and no longer in need of charitable aid. A widely recommended norm to guide one's giving and avoid self-deception is the tithe, the giving of one-tenth of one's income; generally this includes giving to support one's own church as well as to outside charities. This is a guideline, not a law. (It should not be necessary to say something is of grace and not law to the devout evangelicals who most commonly employ this norm, but experience shows that it is.) It should not be treated rigidly: the well off are clearly in a position to give more, and the poor should not be asked to give so much. But for most people of income around the median in affluent countries it is a sound guide.

It cannot be emphasized too strongly that in the biblical perspective such giving is justice. It is not correct to say, as is often done, that it is justice *and not* charity, which implies that there is something called charity which is not justice. To the biblical writers there is no distinction between the two, and *tsedaqa* comes to mean "alms" in later Hebrew. It is justice in the first place because the inhabitants of countries that benefited greatly from the transfer of wealth from colonies to the metropolis owe some return to the inhabitants of those whose countries were plundered. How much would appropriate compensation to Africa for the ruin of the continent by the slave trade come to? Early Christian preachers, taught by the Bible, were clear on this, as for example in the words of John Chrysostom (fourth to fifth century): "Tell me, how is it that you are rich? Who did you get your wealth from? And he, who did he get it from? From his grandfather, he says, and even *his* father. So by climbing way up your family tree are you able to show that you have come by it justly? Of course you cannot: its beginning and root necessarily derive from some injustice." (Chrysostom on 1 Tim. 4; quoted in Miranda 1977: 15, but the translation is mine.) In any case, it is *tsedaqa* for the possessor of wealth to bless the poor and so to continue to receive blessing.

But justice as personal responsibility for those with whom we are personally connected should generally be expressed not just in the giving of money but also in the giving of time and in personal contact. Every locality has its community voluntary groups, and it behoves especially those who have position and power in a locality to give some time, if they have it, and some work, to the assistance of those in need or the development and cultural enrichment of the people. Examples could include working for the Samaritans or in bereavement counselling, or at the Citizens' Advice Bureau, or for a community youth group or for Asylum Welcome; or even an orchestra or dramatic society: it can be something you enjoy! It is true that Christians often experience a high demand on their time from their churches. But their churches should encourage them, if only as an act of witness, to be active in the general community. A church member who is spending less time on the internal activities of a church in order to spend more on the building up of the community or on help for the despairing is doing the work of God – which of course is justice, as the innumerable biblical texts we have looked at testify.

Justice as a Community of Equals

To implement equality requires action on several fronts.

In the first place, in our everyday personal relationships we should treat people as equals. The class-dictated norms of command and deference which have for so long formed and deformed European society may be disappearing, yet it requires positive effort to overcome the legacy of incomprehension, snobbery and resentment which they have left behind. It is sad but true that people in the twenty-first century can still be labelled as "chavs" or "toffs". Americans have never had this problem (and may not know the meaning of the words just quoted!), at least not within white society: race is the problem there, and no less here. Whether it is a question of class, race or gender, it is far more difficult than the idealist may reckon to treat everyone we meet as simply a fellow human creature, to whose eyes God has given light like ourselves (Prov. 29:13) – just as difficult for the presumptively "inferior" as for the supposedly "superior". But for the Creator's sake the effort must be made.

Second, we must once again emphasize that judgement, and justice, begin at the house of God. It is useless for the Church to call for equality in society if the Church itself is no true family of equals. We have already touched on the question of gender equality, but the way in which that question is usually formulated already presumes inequality between clergy and laity. The root question is not whether women can join the clergy, though that is important. It is whether clergy and laity can join on equal terms in the direction of the Church's life. I do not wish to criticize any particular denomination here, but only to say that the Congregational tradition in which I grew up has something to offer the whole church in this respect. This is the seeking of the Lord's will under the guidance of the Holy Spirit in the gathering of the church meeting, in which that guidance may be made known through any member of the gathering, however humble, man or woman, black or white. This is surely in the spirit of what Paul envisaged in urging the "strong" to respect the sensibility of the "weak".

Third, it is necessary to support every effort to make society at the level of the nation more equal, or shall we say less unequal. There are of course many associations in Britain and other advanced societies dedicated to eliminating discrimination against specific groups, fighting for the rights of women, for gays and lesbians, against racial discrimination, for the proper recognition of the needs of people with disabilities. These deserve the support of those who have learnt from the Bible that justice is embodied in a community of equals. Much fewer are those attempting to eliminate inequality altogether. It is interesting that at the time of writing a parliamentary commission in the UK is looking into the question of improving the representation of women and blacks and ethnic minorities in Parliament, yet it does not have on its agenda the better representation of working class people, which has markedly declined in recent years, years of government by the Labour party, which was founded to achieve precisely that. It still does not seem to have sunk in that there is no point in having more women and more black and Asian people in Parliament if they and the white male MPs taken together are only drawn from the top half of a grossly unequal society. But though socialists of the classic mould, people like R. H. Tawney and George Bernard Shaw, conceived of equality as the essence of socialism, it appears that it is no longer an object of the Labour party. Peter Mandelson's notorious comment in 1998 that "we are intensely relaxed about people getting filthy rich" sums it up (even though he did add "as long as they pay their taxes": Mandelson 2008). The appearance of *The Spirit Level* (Wilkinson and Pickett 2009) and the associated founding of The Equality Trust may change this situation. Their website (http://www.equalitytrust.org.uk) offers some actions to take, but the trust is not a membership organization, at least not yet.

What of the inequality of the world community, the colossal disparity in resources, health, education and opportunities between most people in the developed world and the vast majority in less developed nations? What measures need to be, and can be, taken to deal with that? The standard prescription is to tackle "underdevelopment" through aid and trade. And it is true that a number of economies especially in East Asia have moved a long way up the development ladder by judicious investment in export industries. Taiwan, South Korea and Singapore can now be counted as part of the developed world. But they achieved this not by paying attention to the prescriptions of the neo-liberal economists that ruined the former Soviet Union in the 1990s, but by redistributing agricultural land and protecting their fledgling industries until they could fly in the global economy. China, India and Brazil are now having some success in repeating the experiment on a far greater scale.

But quite apart from the inequalities within these countries that this process creates or exacerbates, the plain fact is that the natural resources and carrying capacity of the earth cannot support nine billion people, as the population is projected to be by 2050, at the living standard of the USA, or even the EU, today, even if their rate of carbon use per unit of GDP is 10% of what it is today. Within the constraints imposed by the planet that we all live on, equality, or something approaching it, can only be achieved if many of us move to a lower standard of living, or, more positively expressed, a simpler lifestyle. Specifically, this might mean giving up our cars and our frequent travel, restricting our eating of meat to special occasions, and limiting purchases of consumer goods and services to what we really need. Of course, this implies a contraction of all developed economies, so that it must also involve a redistribution of employment. This must be planned to avoid the misery and bitterness of mass unemployment which is the invariable result of unplanned recession. The contraction would include the export industries in countries like China that provide cheap manufactured goods to the developed world, so that they also must be involved in this plan.

But we are nowhere near that yet! There is a need for both a popular movement and political leadership. Individuals may adopt a simpler lifestyle as a witness, but they should not deceive themselves that this will achieve anything in the short term. As neither such a movement on any large scale nor such leadership appears to exist, I have reached the limit of my practical suggestions for achieving biblical justice. From here on we move into a different mode, inspired by the example of Jesus the suffering Messiah.

Justice as Self-offering

Christians acknowledge as Lord the one who "came not to be served but to serve"; and "the disciple is not greater than the master". The way of servant authority trodden by the Christ is also the way which Christians must tread. We may grant that many of them will find themselves in positions of authority and will wish to use it to establish justice so far as their writ runs, in one of the three modes we have explored. But in the end they will strike against the limits of such dominion, not only the formal limits of their authority but the limits set by the recalcitrance of the human beings they must work with. Moreover, all Christians, however humble and apparently powerless, are called to do the work of God, which is justice, and they are not left without a way of doing it.

I summed this way up at the end of Chapter 6. We might characterize it as modelling justice as distinct from attempting to establish it. And one can only model justice in a community, as Plato saw in writing his *Republic*. But the community of Messianic justice will be very different from Plato's commonwealth. It is a community of equals serving those who are most in need, making themselves at one with the people they serve, and ready if necessary to suffer for them and for the good news of God's just rule; making friends also with those condemned by society and assuring them of God's forgiveness. They will also live life as simply as possible, for the reasons outlined at the end of the last section.

This is the commitment which is asked of any community of the followers of Jesus, and the Church at its best has exemplified these characteristics: even if it has been rare for all of them to be exhibited at the same time in one community, at least some of them may be found in some communities at most periods. But the tendency has always been for churches to lose sight of this commitment, developing hierarchies, making friends with the powerful, dominating the vulnerable rather than serving them, demanding the observance of rules for their own sake rather than for the sake of people (cf. Mark 2:27), and dispensing forgiveness according to a tariff. This has especially been the result of the acceptance and promotion of Christianity by rulers. But even so, we have to admit that many of the unchristian characteristics of the Church can develop and have developed even under persecution.

The result has been, at many periods, that communities have been formed largely independent of the formal structures of the Church in order to pursue the Christian virtues more single-mindedly. The precise virtues aimed at have varied, and have not necessarily been in all respects the same as those listed above. The monastic movement, from its beginnings in fourth-century Egypt, has set great store by celibacy as well as poverty; obedience was added once it became expressed in organized communities. But its central purpose has been the praise of God and the cultivation of the soul rather than the pursuit of justice in human society. The Franciscan movement in its origins came closer to what I have in mind. Its central purpose was the preaching of the gospel to the poor, and its members, the Friars Minor or "little brothers", strove to live at one with the poor, dressing in the peasant's coarse gown, owning no property and living by begging.

The adoption of the name "brothers" in itself signified the equality of the members.

At the present day there are a wide range of Christian communities and individuals seeking to live alongside the poor and serve them, to fight for justice for them, and to live simply. Some are residential communities living in common and working full time for the community's objects; others consist of people living and gaining a livelihood in the world while committed to those objects so far as they are able.

We may mention the base communities of the Catholic Church in Latin America, which are communities of actual poor people, with some leadership, living in poor areas, who join in worship and biblical reflection and work for the good of the area and its people, often in opposition to powerful interests.

In the UK, the Iona Community, founded by George MacLeod, includes ministers and lay people living in the world but united by a common rule, which includes daily prayer and Bible reading, "mutual sharing and accountability for the use of our time and money" (which must be a strong incentive to simplicity), regular meeting together, and "action and reflection for justice, peace and the integrity of creation" (Iona Community 2009; see also Ferguson 1998). Members of the Iona Community may live anywhere, and most, apart from those working at its centres in Glasgow and on Iona, will find themselves living and acting alongside non-members with only long-range and periodic support from fellow-members. More locally concentrated examples are provided by the ventures founded by John Vincent, including the Urban Theology Unit in Sheffield and the Ashram Community. The ethos of these ventures is commitment to the gospel of the kingdom of God understood in radical political terms, and to the people of the inner city and their struggles. This is expressed in UTU through the study of theology as a practical discipline learned in work alongside the people of Sheffield, or wherever participants may live, and in the Ashram Community in mutual sharing of worship, food and life and the practice of hospitality (Duffield *et al.* 2000; Urban Theology Unit 2009; Vincent 1992; Ashram Community 2009). All members of the Ashram Community commit themselves, among other things, "to offer the Kingdom in political and economic witness, to work for the new community of all creation, and to risk ourselves in a lifestyle of sharing" (Ashram Community 2009). Not all members live in an Ashram House, but many do, working in the local community, and others commit themselves to regular meeting; many are active in community work in the inner city.

Many other examples could be cited, but these may be enough to show that the serious attempt to live for God's justice as followers of Jesus is a living and effective option in the world today. It is worth repeating that for all the commitment and integrity of these communities, their effectiveness or success is not to be measured by the changes that take place around them in the course of a few years. Their object should rather be understood as a witness to the justice of God's kingdom in a world whose whole nature and *raison d'être* is hostile to it. That is not to say that the witness has no practical effect. On the contrary, if faithfully maintained it may ultimately work revolutions – but patience is essential. The opposite errors of despair and utopianism both arise from forgetting that the world is recalcitrant to the justice of God and that the victory is God's and not ours. Yet God's justice is embodied in human justice, in all the various ways that we have explored in this book, and our practical witness to God's incarnate justice in Jesus Christ in itself embodies and achieves that justice.

BIBLIOGRAPHY

Alexamenos graffito. 2009. http://en.wikipedia.org/wiki/Alexamenos_graffito (accessed 27 November 2009).

Aristotle. 1939. *The Nicomachean Ethics*, trans., H. Rackham (LCL). London: Heinemann.

——— 2000. *Politics*, trans., Benjamin Jowett, with intro., etc. by H. W. C. Davis. Mineola, NY: Dover Publications (Reprint of 1905 edition, Oxford: Oxford University Press).

Ashram Community. 2009. http://www.ashram.org.uk

Barrett, C. K. 1968. *A Commentary on the First Epistle to the Corinthians.* London: A. & C. Black.

Barton, John. 1979. "Natural Law and Poetic Justice in the Old Testament." *Journal of Theological Studies* 30: 1–14.

——— 1980. *Amos' Oracles against the Nations. A Study of Amos 1.3–2.5* (SOTSMS 6). Cambridge: Cambridge University Press.

——— 2003. *Understanding Old Testament Ethics: Approaches and Explorations.* Louisville, KY: Westminster John Knox.

Bauckham, Richard. 1993. *The Climax of Prophecy: Studies on the Book of Revelation.* Edinburgh: T & T Clark.

——— 2010. *Bible and Ecology: Rediscovering the Community of Creation.* London: Darton, Longman and Todd.

Bendor, S. 1996. *The Social Structure of Ancient Israel: The Institution of the Family (Beit 'Ab) from the Settlement to the End of the Monarchy.* Jerusalem Biblical Studies, 7; Jerusalem: Simor.

Bennett, Harold V. 2002. *Injustice Made Legal: Deuteronomic Law and the Plight of Widows, Strangers and Orphans in Ancient Israel.* Grand Rapids, MI: Eerdmans.

Birch, Bruce C. 1995. "Divine Character and the Formation of Moral Community in the Book of Exodus." In Rogerson, Davies and Carroll 1995: 119–35.

Bondi, R. 1984. "The Elements of Character." *Journal of Religious Ethics* 12: 201–18.

Boring, M. Eugene. 2006. *Mark: A Commentary.* Louisville, KY: Westminster John Knox.

Brueggemann, Walter. 1994. "Theodicy in a Social Dimension." In *A Social Reading of the Old Testament: Prophetic Approaches to Israel's Communal Life*, ed. Patrick D. Miller: 174-96. Minneapolis, MN: Fortress Press.

—— 1995. "Pharaoh as a Vassal: A Study of a Political Metaphor." *Catholic Biblical Quarterly* 57: 27–51.

Caird, G. B. 1966. *The Revelation of St John the Divine.* London: A & C Black.

Calvin, John. 1854. *Commentary on the Four Last Books of Moses, Arranged in the Form of a Harmony*, trans. C. W. Bingham. 4 vols. Edinburgh: Calvin Translation Society.

Carroll, R., Mark Daniel. 1992. *Contexts for Amos: Prophetic Poetics in Latin American Perspective.* Sheffield: JSOT Press.

Carter, Charles E. 1999. *The Emergence of Yehud in the Persian Period: A Social and Demographic Study* (JSOTSup, 294). Sheffield: Sheffield Academic Press.

Charity Commission 2009. www.charitycommission.gov.uk.../ CharityNumbers1105851 (Christian Aid), 202918 (Oxfam). Accessed 31 March 2009.

Childs, Brevard S. 1974. *Exodus: A Commentary.* London: SCM Press.

Chirichigno, Gregory C. 1993. *Debt-Slavery in Israel and the Ancient Near East* (JSOTSup, 141). Sheffield: JSOT Press.

Chrysostom, John on 1 Tim. 4. In Epistulam I ad Timotheum Cap. IV, Homilia 12. *PG* 62: 562–63.

Clark, Gordon R. 1993. *The Word* Hesed *in the Hebrew Bible.* Sheffield: JSOT Press.

Clines, David J. A. 1978, 1997. *The Theme of the Pentateuch.* Sheffield: JSOT Press/Sheffield Academic Press.

—— 1990. "What Does Eve Do to Help?" In *What Does Eve Do to Help? and Other Readerly Questions to the Old Testament.* D. J. A. Clines: 25-48. Sheffield: JSOT Press.

Coats, George W. 1977. "The King's Loyal Opposition: Obedience and Authority in Exodus 32–34." In *Canon and Authority: Essays in Old Testament Religion and Theology*, eds George W. Coats and Burke O. Long: 91–109. Philadelphia, PA: Fortress Press.

Coote, Robert B. 1981. *Amos among the Prophets.* Philadelphia, PA: Fortress Press.

Cranfield, C. E. B. 1963. *The Gospel According to Saint Mark.* Second impression with supplementary notes. Cambridge: Cambridge University Press.

Croatto, José Severino. 1981. *Exodus: A Hermeneutics of Freedom.* Maryknoll, NY: Orbis Books; ET of *Liberación y libertad.*

Crossley, James G. 2005. "The Damned Rich (Mark 10:17–31)." *The Expository Times* 116: 397–401.

—— 2009. "Mark 7.1–23: Revisiting the Question of 'All Foods Clean.'" In *Torah in the New Testament: Papers Delivered at the Manchester-Lausanne Seminar of June 2008* (LNTS 401), eds Michael Tait and Peter Oakes, 8-20. London: T&T Clark International.

Davies, Margaret. 1995. "Work and Slavery in the New Testament: Impoverishments of Traditions." In Rogerson, Davies and Carroll R. 1995, 315–47.

De Geus, C. H. J. 2003. *Towns in Ancient Israel and in the Southern Levant.* Leuven: Peeters.

Derrett, J. Duncan M. 1972. "'Take thy bond … and write fifty' (Lk xvi.6). The nature of the bond." *Journal of Theological Studies* NS 23: 438–40.

Dickens, Charles. n.d. *Sketches By "Boz"*. London: Miles and Miles.

Dickerson, S. S. and M. E. Kemeny. 2004. "Acute stressors and cortisol responses: a theoretical integration and synthesis of laboratory research." *Psychological Bulletin* 130: 355–91.

Downing, F. Gerald. 2010. "Ambiguity, Ancient Semantics, and Faith." *New Testament Studies* 56: 139–62.

Duffield, Ian K., Christine Jones and John Vincent. 2000. *Crucibles: Creating Theology at UTU*. Sheffield: Urban Theology Unit.

Dunn, James D. G. 1988. *Romans 1-8; Romans 9-12* (WBC 38A, B). Dallas, TX: Word Books.

Dunn, John. 2005. *Setting the People Free: The Story of Democracy*. London: Atlantic Books.

Durham, John I. 1987. *Exodus* (Word Biblical Commentary, 3). Waco, TX: Word Books.

Eisenstadt, S. N. and L. Roniger. 1984. *Patrons, Clients and Friends: Interpersonal Relations and the Structure of Trust in Society*. Cambridge: Cambridge University Press.

Eskenazi, Tamara Cohn. 2006. "The Missions of Ezra and Nehemiah." In Lipschits and Oeming (eds) 2006: 509–30.

Faust, Avraham. 1999a. "Differences in Family Structure between Cities and Villages in Iron Age II." *Tel Aviv* 26: 233–52.

——— 1999b. "Socioeconomic Stratification in an Israelite City: Hazor VI as a Test Case." *Levant* 31: 179–90.

——— 2000. "The Rural Community in Ancient Israel during Iron Age II." *Bulletin of the American Schools of Oriental Research* 317: 17–39.

——— 2003. "Judah in the Sixth Century BCE: A Rural Perspective." *Palestine Exploration Quarterly* 135: 37–53.

——— 2004. "'Mortuary Practices, Society and Ideology': The Lack of Iron Age I Burials in the Highlands in Context." *Israel Exploration Journal* 54: 174–90.

——— 2005. "The Settlement of Jerusalem's Western Hill and the City's Status in Iron Age II Revisited." *Zeitschrift des Deutschen Palästina-Vereins* 121: 97–118.

——— forthcoming. *Israelite Society in the Period of the Monarchy: An Archaeological Investigation* (or similar title). Winona Lake, IN: Eisenbrauns. This translation of Faust's 2005 book in Hebrew will include most of the details in the above articles.

Ferguson, Ron. 1998. *Chasing the Wild Goose: The Story of the Iona Community*. Glasgow: Wild Goose Publications.

Fretheim, Terence E. 2005. *God and World in the Old Testament: A Relational Theology of Creation*. Nashville, TN: Abingdon Press.

Freyne, Sean. 1980. *Galilee from Alexander the Great to Hadrian, 323 BCE to 135 CE*. Wilmington, DE: Michael Glazier. Reprinted Edinburgh: T & T Clark, 1998.

Friesen, Steven J. 2004. "Poverty in Pauline Studies: Beyond the So-called New Consensus". *Journal for the Study of the New Testament* 26 (3): 323–61.

Fritz, Volkmar. 1995. *The City in Ancient Israel*. Sheffield: Sheffield Academic Press.

Gadamer, Hans-Georg. 1989. *Truth and Method*. Second edition. London: Sheed & Ward. (ET of *Wahrheit und Methode*; fifth German edition in *Gesammelte Werke*, I. Tübingen: Mohr, 1986.)

Galbraith, John Kenneth. 1958. *The Affluent Society*. London: Hamish Hamilton.

Goodman, Martin. 2008. *Rome and Jerusalem: The Clash of Ancient Civilizations*. London: Penguin.

Gorringe, Timothy. 1994. *Capital and the Kingdom: Theological Ethics and Economic Order*. London: SPCK and Maryknoll, NY: Orbis.

Gowan, Donald M. 1994. *Theology in Exodus*. Louisville, KY: Westminster John Knox.

Grabbe, Lester L. 2006. "The 'Persian Documents' in the Book of Ezra: Are They Authentic?" In Lipschits and Oeming (eds) 2006: 531–70.

——— 2007. *Ancient Israel: What Do We Know and How Do We Know It?* London: T & T Clark.

Guardian. 2009. http://www.guardian.co.uk/news/datablog/2009/mar/09/economicgrowth-economy (Accessed 27 October 2009.)

Gunkel, Hermann. 1997. *Genesis*. Macon, GA: Mercer University Press. (ET of *Genesis, übersetzt und erklärt*. Third edition. Göttingen: Vandenhoeck und Ruprecht, 1910.)

Gunn, David M. 1982. "The Hardening of Pharaoh's Heart." In *Art and Meaning: Rhetoric in Biblical Literature*, eds David J. A. Clines, David M. Gunn and Alan Hauser: 72–96. Sheffield: Sheffield Academic Press.

Gutiérrez, Gustavo. 1988. *A Theology of Liberation*. Second edition. London: SCM Press. (Revised ET of *Teología de liberación*. Lima: Centro de Estudios y Publicaciones, 1971.)

Habel, Norman C. 1995. *The Land Is Mine: Six Biblical Land Ideologies*. Minneapolis, MN: Fortress.

Haenchen, Ernst. 1971. *The Acts of the Apostles: A Commentary*. Oxford: Blackwell. (Translation of 14th German edition, 1965.)

Hamilton, Jeffries M. 1992. *Social Justice and Deuteronomy: The Case of Deuteronomy 15*. Atlanta, GA: Scholars Press.

Hauerwas, Stanley. 1981. *A Community of Character*. Notre Dame, IN: University of Notre Dame Press.

Horrell, David G. 2001. "From ἀδελφοί to οἶκος θεοῦ: Social Transformation in Pauline Christianity." *Journal of Biblical Literature* 120: 293–311.

——— 2005. *Solidarity and Difference: A Contemporary Reading of Paul's Ethics*, London: T & T Clark International.

——— 2010. *The Bible and the Environment: Towards a Critical Ecological Biblical Theology*. London: Equinox.

Horsley, Richard A. and John S. Hanson. 1985. *Bandits, Prophets and Messiahs: Popular Movements in the Time of Jesus*. Minneapolis, MN: Winston Press. Reprinted San Francisco, CA: Harper & Row, 1988.

Houston, Walter 1993. *Purity and Monotheism: Clean and Unclean Animals in Biblical Law*. Sheffield: Sheffield Academic Press.

—— 1995. "'You shall open your hand to your needy brother': Ideology and Moral Formation in Deut. 15.1–18." In Rogerson, Davies and Carroll, 1995: 296–314.

—— 1999. "The King's Preferential Option for the Poor: Rhetoric, Ideology and Ethics in Psalm 72." *Biblical Interpretaion* 7: 341–67.

—— 2001a. "Exodus." In *The Oxford Bible Commentary*, eds John Barton and John Muddiman: 67–91. Oxford: Oxford University Press.

—— 2001b. "What's Just about the Jubilee?" *Studies in Christian Ethics* 14 (1): 34–47.

Houston, Walter J. 2007. "The Character of YHWH and the Ethics of the Hebrew Bible: Is *Imitatio Dei* a Safe Principle?" *Journal of Theological Studies* 58: 1–25.

—— 2008. *Contending for Justice*. Second edition. London: T & T Clark.

—— 2010. "Justice and Violence in the Priestly Utopia." In *Bible and Justice: Ancient Texts, Modern Challenges*, ed. Matthew J. M. Coomber. London: Equinox.

Hutton, Will. 1995. *The State We're In*. London: Cape.

Iona Community. 2009. http://www.iona.org.uk/iona_community.php

Jackson, Bernard S. 1989. "Ideas of law and legal administration: a semiotic approach." In *The World of Ancient Israel: Sociological, Anthropological and Political Perspectives*, ed. R. E. Clements: 185–202. Cambridge: Cambridge University Press.

—— 2006. *Wisdom-Laws: A Study of the Mishpatim of Exodus 21:1–22:16*. Oxford: Oxford University Press.

Jackson, Tim. 2009. *Prosperity Without Growth: Economics for a Finite Planet*. London: Earthscan.

Jeremias, Joachim. 1969. *Jerusalem in the Time of Jesus*. ET of *Jerusalem zur Zeit Jesu*. Third edition. Göttingen: Vandenhoeck & Ruprecht, 1962.

Kaminsky, Joel S. 1995. *Corporate Responsibility in the Hebrew Bible*. Sheffield: Sheffield Academic Press.

Kippenberg, Hans G. 1982. *Religion und Klassenbildung im antiken Judäa*. Second edition. Göttingen: Vandenhoeck & Ruprecht.

Knierim, Rolf P. 1995. "Justice in Old Testament Theology", in "The Interpretation of the Old Testament." In *The Task of Old Testament Theology*, R. P. Knierim: 86-122. Grand Rapids, MI: Eerdmans.

Kovacs, Brian W. 1974. "Is There a Class-Ethic in Proverbs?" In *Essays in Old Testament Ethics*, eds J. L. Crenshaw and J. T. Willis: 173–89. New York: Ktav.

Lang, Bernhard. 1985. "The Social Organization of Peasant Poverty in Biblical Israel." In *Anthropological Approaches to the Old Testament*, B. Lang (ed.): 83–99. London: SPCK. Reprinted from Bernhard Lang, *Monotheism and the Prophetic Minority*: 114-27. SWBA, 1; Sheffield: Almond Press, 1983.

Layard, Richard. 2005. *Happiness: Lessons from a New Science*. London: Allen Lane.

Lefebvre, Jean-François. 2003. *Le jubilé biblique: Lv 25—exégèse et théologie.* Fribourg Suisse: Editions Universitaires/Göttingen: Vandenhoeck & Ruprecht.

Lenski, Gerhard E. 1966. *Power and Privilege: A Theory of Social Stratification.* New York: McGraw-Hill.

Levenson, Jon D. 1993. "Exodus and Liberation." In *The Hebrew Bible, the Old Testament and Historical Criticism: Jews and Christians in Biblical Studies,* J. D. Levenson: 127–59. Louisville, KY: Westminster John Knox.

Lipschits, Oded. 2003. "Demographic Changes in Judah between the Seventh and the Fifth Centuries B.C.E." In *Judah and the Judeans in the Neo-Babylonian Period,* eds O. Lipschits and Joseph Blenkinsopp: 323–76. Winona Lake, IN: Eisenbrauns.

Lipschits, Oded and Manfred Oeming (eds) 2006. *Judah and the Judeans in the Persian Period.* Winona Lake: Eisenbrauns.

Mandelson, Peter. 2008. Letter, *The Guardian,* Saturday 12 January.

Marlow, Hilary. 2009. *Biblical Prophets and Contemporary Environmental Ethics.* Oxford: Oxford University Press.

Marx, Karl. 1959 (1894). *Capital: A Critique of Political Economy,* vol. 3, ed. Frederick Engels. London: Lawrence & Wishart.

McCarthy, D. J. 1972. *Old Testament Covenant. A Survey of Current Opinions.* Oxford: Blackwell.

McNutt, Paula M. 1999. *Reconstructing the Society of Ancient Israel.* London: SPCK/Louisville, KY: Westminster John Knox.

Meeks, Wayne A. 1983. *The First Urban Christians: The Social World of the Apostle Paul.* New Haven, CT: Yale.

Meggitt, Justin J. 1998. *Paul, Poverty and Survival.* Edinburgh: T & T Clark.

Mendenhall, G. E. 1954. "Covenant Forms in Israelite Tradition." *Biblical Archaeology* 17: 50–76.

Meyers, Carol. 1988. *Discovering Eve: Ancient Israelite Women in Context.* New York/Oxford: Oxford University Press.

Middlemas, Jill. 2005. *The Troubles of Templeless Judah.* Oxford: University Press.

Milanovic, Branko. 2002. "True world income distribution, 1988 and 1993: First calculation based on household surveys alone." *Economic Journal,* 112 (476, January): 1–56.

Milgrom, Jacob. 2000. *Leviticus 17–22: A New Translation with Introduction and Commentary* (AB, 3A). New York: Doubleday.

Mingo Kaminouchi, Alberto de. 2003. *"But it is Not So Among You": Echoes of Power in Mark 10.32–45.* London/New York: T & T Clark International.

Miranda, José Porfirio. 1977. *Marx and the Bible: A Critique of the Philosophy of Oppression.* London: SCM Press. (ET of *Marx y la biblia: Critica a ls filosofia de la opresión.* Salamanca: Ediciones Sigueme: 1971.)

Moberly, R. W. L. 1983. *At the Mountain of God: Story and Theology in Exodus 32–34.* Sheffield: JSOT Press.

Monbiot, George. 2006. *Heat: How to Stop the Planet Burning.* London: Allen Lane.

Mosala, Itumeleng J. 1989. *Biblical Hermeneutics and Black Theology in South Africa*. Grand Rapids, MI: Eerdmans.

Myers, Ched. 1988. *Binding the Strong Man: A Political Reading of Mark's Story of Jesus*. Maryknoll, NY: Orbis.

Nelson, Richard D. 2002. *Deuteronomy: A Commentary*. Louisville, KY: Westminster John Knox.

Newsom, Carol A. 2003. *The Book of Job: A Contest of Moral Imaginations*. New York: Oxford University Press.

Nicholson, Ernest W. 1986. *God and His People: Covenant and Theology in the Old Testament*. Oxford: Clarendon Press.

Nolan, Peter. 2009. Address to Friends of the Church in China, 28 November.

O'Donovan, Oliver and Joan Lockwood O'Donovan (eds). 1999. *From Irenaeus to Grotius: A Sourcebook in Christian Political Thought 100–1625*. Grand Rapids, MI: Eerdmans.

ONS (Office of National Statistics). 2009. *Executive Summary: Wealth in Great Britain 2006–2008.pdf*. Available at http://www.statistics.gov.uk/StatBase/Product.asp?vlnk=15074

Perdue, Leo G., Joseph Blenkinsopp, John J. Collins and Carol Meyers. 1997. *Families in Ancient Israel*. Louisville, KY: Westminster John Knox.

Perlitt, Lothar. 1980. "Ein einzig Volk von Brüdern." In *Kirche: Festschrift für Günther Bornkamm zum 75 Geburtstag*, eds D. Lührmann and G. Strecker: 27–52. Tübingen: Mohr.

Pilch, John J. and Bruce J. Malina (eds). 1998. *Handbook of Biblical Social Values*. Second edition. Peabody, MA: Hendrickson.

Pleins, David J. 2001. *The Social Visions of the Hebrew Bible*. Louisville, KY: Westminster John Knox Press.

Preston, R. H. 1976. "Introduction". In William Temple, *Christianity and Social Order*: 5-26. (First edition reprinted). London: Shepheard-Walwyn, SPCK.

Propp, William H. C. 2006. *Exodus 19–40: A New Translation with Introduction and Commentary* (Anchor Bible 2A). New York: Doubleday.

Rawls, John. 1971. *A Theory of Justice*. Cambridge, MA: Belknap.

—— 2001. *Justice as Fairness: A Restatement*. Cambridge, MA: Belknap.

Reimer, David J. 1996. "The Apocrypha and Biblical Theology: The Case of Interpersonal Forgiveness." In *After the Exile: Essays in Honour of Rex Mason*, eds John Barton and David J. Reimer: 259–82. Macon, GA: Mercer University Press.

Richardson, M. E. J. 2000. *Hammurabi's Laws: Text, Translation and Glossary*. Sheffield: Sheffield Academic Press.

Rodd, Cyril S. 2001. *Glimpses of a Strange Land: Studies in Old Testament Ethics*. Edinburgh: T & T Clark.

Rogerson, J. W. 1991. *Genesis 1–11* (Old Testament Guides). Sheffield: JSOT Press.

—— 2007. *According to the Scriptures: The Challenge of Using the Bible in Social, Moral and Political Questions* (Biblical Challenges in the Contemporary World). London: Equinox.

—— 2009. *A Theology of the Old Testament: Cultural Memory, Communication and Being Human*. London: SPCK.

Rogerson, J. W. and John Vincent. 2009. *The City in Biblical Perspective* (Biblical Challenges in the Contemporary World). London: Equinox.

Rogerson, John W., Margaret Davies and M. Daniel Carroll R. (eds). 1995. *The Bible in Ethics: The Second Sheffield Colloquium*. Sheffield: Sheffield Academic Press.

Sandel, Michael J. 2009. *Justice: What's the Right Thing to Do?* London: Allen Lane.

Sanders, E. P. 1985. *Jesus and Judaism*. London: SCM Press.

Schluter, Michael and Roy Clements. 1986, *Reactivating the Extended Family: From Biblical Norms to Public Policy in Britain*. Cambridge: Jubilee Centre.

Sen, Amartya. 2009. *The Idea of Justice*. London: Allen Lane.

Simkins, Ronald A. 1999. "Patronage and the Political Economy of Monarchic Israel." *Semeia* 87: 123–44.

Sloane, Andrew. 2008. *At Home in a Strange Land: Using the Old Testament in Christian Ethics*. Peabody, MA: Hendrickson.

Stiglitz, Joseph E. 2002. *Globalization and its Discontents*. London: Penguin.

Tawney, R. H. 1964 [1935]. *Equality* (with a new introduction by Richard M. Titmuss). London: Allen and Unwin.

Taylor, Vincent. 1952. *The Gospel According to St. Mark: The Greek Text with Introduction, Notes and Indexes*. London: Macmillan.

Temple, William. 1941. "Opening address." In *Malvern, 1941. The Life of the Church and the Order of Society: being the Proceedings of the Archbishop of York's Conference*: 9–15. London: Longmans Green.

Theissen, Gerd. 1982. *The Social Setting of Pauline Christianity: Essays on Corinth*. Edinburgh: T & T Clark.

Tocqueville, Alexis de. 2003. *Democracy in America; and Two Essays on America*, trans. G. E. Bevan. London: Penguin.

Twenge, J. M. 2007. "The age of anxiety? Birth cohort change in anxiety and neuroticism." *Journal of Personality and Social Psychology* 79: 1007–21.

United Nations. 2000. General Assembly, 55th session, Resolution 2: UN Millennium Declaration. http://www.un.org/Depts/dhl/resguide/r55.htm Accessed as pdf 26 October 2009.

UNU-WIDER. 2006. http://www.wider.unu.edu/events/past-events/2006-events/en_GB/05-12-2006 Accessed 26 October 2009.

Urban Theology Unit. 2009. http://www.utusheffield.org.uk

US Department of Justice. 2002. http://ojp.usdoj.gov/bjs/reentry/recidivism.htm Accessed 26 October 2009.

Vermes, Geza. 1995. *The Dead Sea Scrolls in English*. Fourth edition. London: Penguin Books.

Vincent, John J. (ed.). 1992. *A Community Called Ashram*. Sheffield: Ashram Community Trust.

Walzer, Michael. 1987. *Interpretation and Social Criticism*. Cambridge, MA: Harvard University Press.

Wasow, Bernard, Matt Homer, Elah Lanis and Jonah Liebert. 2008. "Going Nowhere: Workers' Wages since the Mid-1970s" (GoingNowhereRC.pdf). http://www.tcf.org/list.asp?type=PB&pubid=482: website of The Century Foundation. Accessed on 27 October 2009.

Weber, Max. 1952. *Ancient Judaism*. Glencoe, IL: The Free Press. (ET of *Das antike Judentum*, Tübingen 1921.)

Weinberg, Joel P. 1992. *The Citizen-Temple Community*. JSOTSup, 151. Sheffield: JSOT Press.

Weinfeld, Moshe. 1995. *Social Justice in Ancient Israel and in the Ancient Near East*. Jerusalem: The Magnes Press/Minneapolis, MN: Fortress Press.

Wijk-Bos, Johanna W. H. van. 2005. *Making Wise the Simple: The Torah in Christian Faith and Practice*. Grand Rapids, MI: Eerdmans.

Wilkinson, Richard, and Kate Pickett. 2009. *The Spirit Level: Why More Equal Societies Almost Always Do Better*. London: Allen Lane.

Wolf, Eric R. 1966. *Peasants*. Englewood Cliffs, NJ: Prentice-Hall.

Wolfe, Tom. 1988. *The Bonfire of the Vanities*. London: Cape.

Wright, Addison G. 1982. "The Widow's Mites: Praise or Lament? – A Matter of Context." *Catholic Biblical Quarterly* 44: 256–65.

Wright, Christopher J. H. 1990. *God's People in God's Land: Family, Land and Property in the Old Testament*. Grand Rapids, MI: Eerdmans/Exeter: Paternoster Press.

—— 2004. *Old Testament Ethics for the People of God*. Leicester: Inter-Varsity Press.

Zimmerli, Walter. 1968. "Das zweite Gebot." In *Gottes Offenbarung*, W. Zimmerli: 234–48. Munich: Kaiser.

Index of biblical texts
References are to the English Bible

Index of subjects

For proper names see the Index of Names

INDEX OF NAMES

This index includes all authors referred to in the text,
and a selection of other proper names